Homeowners,

It's Time to Think Like a

General Contractor

By

David M. Dillon

General Contractor

Residential New Construction and Renovation

Note: This book is a compilation of the opinions of the author on the subject matter and is not intended to offer professional services. It is strongly encouraged for any reader in need of advice to seek it from local professional experts. The author and publisher cannot assume any responsibility for damage to property and/or injury to persons, loss of profits, loss of revenue to a customer or third party as the result of use or misuse of information provided in this publication. The author and publisher make no implied warranties or guarantees as to the completeness and accuracy of the information in this publication. Always consult your local building and zoning department to clarify requirements for licenses, building codes, permit requirements and any local laws concerning construction and design-related issues. The concepts and techniques described in this publication are general. Other techniques not shown in this publication may be necessary. Use good judgment and caution in approaching any design or construction project and consult with professional experts when necessary.

Cover Design by David M. Dillon

For every homeowner who simply wants a more comfortable place to live, *you* are the solution

CONTENT

Preface

By the time you finish this sentence, thousands of people from coast to coast will have seriously agonized over their home improvement project, some even to the point of affecting their health. They plunged headlong into a seemingly simple endeavor to make their home more comfortable, only to be ensnared by a complex web of contractor schemes and their own costly mistakes that separate even the shrewd from their money and leaves them gasping for relief from what amounted to an unexpected nightmarish experience. Some knew so little about the process of home improvement, just about everything shook them up emotionally. That bothers me immensely and we'll spend a considerable amount of time on how to prevent this all too common experience from ever happening...long before it starts.

There's a dark, inside game to every industry and if you're not an insider, you're simply a potential victim. We'll explore the insider's perspective of General Contracting in great detail so that any homeowner can be protected from being mislead and play a much more productive and informed role in their own home improvement. Your best advocate, the only one you can truly trust is *yourself*. We'll uncover how *you* can personally and confidently take charge of any sized project and manage it from start to finish to achieve excellence. Ignorance can be costly and painful in a home improvement project and I see homeowners cost themselves money and unnecessary anguish all too frequently because of their lack of knowledge. I see it all the time and I also hear their horrific contractor stories from the past. I fix their problems. I only wish they had called me first.

A note from the author

The desire to write this book was the result of looking into people's eyes over the years as I sat in their living rooms and at their kitchen tables and listened to their genuinely excited aspirations to improve their homes. Those countless discussions spanned everything from replacing an outdated bathroom vanity to tearing down a neglected old house to make room for a 10,000 square foot, 6 bedroom, 10 bathroom masterpiece. I managed those two projects from start to finish and just about everything in between, but I certainly haven't seen it all yet--not even close. Every project is different. Every project has its own challenges and satisfactions and there is always more to learn. Always.

I have, however, seen my fair share of homeowner's highly emotional reactions as they waded deeper into the renovation or construction of their home and were caught off guard and stunned by their own misconceptions about the process. It's not entirely their fault, mind you. They don't do this for a living, so they can't be expected to thoroughly understand the subtleties if they don't experience it every day. However, there are times when logic and rational thinking seem to be in short supply.

I understood their misconceptions were pure and innocent and I sincerely empathized with them, but their occasional frazzled melt downs were very real and very stressful for them and that bothered me, a lot, as a human being. It's just not healthy. I watched people literally burst into tears or completely lose their composure in profanity-laced tirades over something that was actually progressing quite well, exactly as planned, precisely as discussed and perfectly on track. They would all apologize the next day after realizing everything was fine and you sort of grew used to that cycle, but you also longed for a cure to prevent it altogether, for everyone's sake...

I also saw plenty of irrational decisions by homeowners in the middle of the project. These decisions would derail the momentum and tack on additional weeks to the project and not actually improve anything at all, in spite of additional costs. This caused my clients more unnecessary stress and more money as we drifted past target completion dates because of the multitude of changes they suddenly insisted on after we started construction. You would wonder why things would only come up *after* you started the construction and not in the months leading up to it during the careful, meticulous design meetings, but it happens. Then, they have dinner with some friends, their friends give them advice and the next thing you know, you're tearing out something you installed a week ago. It happens, more often than you would think, just that fast. You shake your head and persevere through it, always accommodating their requests, no matter how ill-advised they were. It's their house, it's their call and you're there to answer that call and get it done.

As a General Contractor, you should always be open to making some adjustments to the design during construction to improve it, which is very normal. But, there were moments when a client would change the design a dozen different times in a 2-3 day period *during* the construction phase and that becomes an all out logistical nightmare. You think you're confirmed on everything and ready to keep building when the client has an "epiphany." So, you stop everything and start identifying how many subcontractors will be affected by this "new direction" in the game plan because everything is so interrelated in construction. It also generates an avalanche of contractual changes which need to be cleared up and signed off on before you can go forward. By the time you chase that down and clean up all the contracts, some clients, you guessed it, have another "epiphany" or just simply change their mind back to the original plan. So, you start the paperwork avalanche all over again. This kind of repetitive stop and start decision making always does more harm than good and is purely the result of someone not really knowing what they're doing.

You start to daydream about creating a weekend "Homeowners Boot Camp" where you could carefully prepare them mentally, logistically and practically on the process of construction. The only problem being... too many homeowners think they could skip something useful like this. Many think that since they remodeled a family room in their previous house, many years ago, they are battle-tested veterans of all things construction. You really wish they were veterans, but quickly find out just the opposite. They often know just enough to be dangerous...and are poised to make that abundantly clear, just a few days into the build.

If only they could genuinely understand some very basic concepts of construction, it would be so much easier on them and so much more fun! You wonder what it would be like if the homeowner managed the entire project themselves and you're convinced that they would at least be more laser focused, more genuinely helpful, more productive and much more decisive. Knowing this is far-fetched for most of them, you wonder how much more smoothly the project would go if they could just merely *Think like a General Contractor* as they made decisions. That alone, would be an incredibly helpful mindset for them to have going into the build out. It would make a world of difference!

Affluence, or lack thereof had no bearing on how well people navigated the construction stage. I've managed projects in neighborhoods where you could easily get shot, for real, in the daytime... I've also worked in neighborhoods with a very legitimate danger of getting flattened by a new Ranger Rover driven by somebody glancing down at a text message. I've managed projects for people who were unemployed for months on end. Some were retired. Others owned their own companies and had houses all over the world. Some of my clients drove a Bentley. Some drove a Ferrari. Some had their own personal chef, an airplane, a yacht. One actually owned an island, no, make that two islands.

No matter what their socioeconomic "rank" in life was, they all wanted the best for their homes and insisted on top notch quality and I respected that and delivered nothing less. Every single one of them was an intelligent, capable individual with good intentions. However, most of them were at one time or another, *way* over their head during the project and as lost as a missing toddler in a shopping mall. This, mind you, was *in spite of* countless discussions to clarify *exactly* what would happen and when. That continues to baffle me, but I blame myself for not apparently explaining things clearly enough, right? But how? Is it really me? Do they really listen? What gives here? Why is there always a burning desire to get started, but never the same burning desire to clearly understand what we're about to do to their house? Is it the whole "instant gratification" factor influencing everything these days?

In addition to that riddle, there is an ever present disconnect on the all important concept of cost. My phone rings all the time with homeowners extremely interested in projects that they simply can't afford. Don't get me wrong, I'm always grateful for the opportunity to discuss a potential project, but I have *way* too many conversations with people about projects they simply can't afford--by a wide margin, and they're in denial about it too. They might as well be shopping for a brand new air craft carrier. They are just as likely to afford one of those as they are adding a second floor to their house, with a budget that would maybe cover the lumber for a tree fort. A small tree fort.

When I quickly break down how their renovation goals could easily exceed their modest budget, they are perplexed. When I suggest very specific ways to trim costs, maintain quality, consider managing it themselves and to try to do it in phases, I might as well be speaking another language. They are equally perplexed. I really want to help them, but a quick dose of honest advice from me only makes them more eager to call the next GC on their list in the hopes that he'll do it all for the budget they can afford. Some homeowners eventually "get it" and call me back months later after they do some more due diligence. Others sign a contract with some slick talking GC that is worded so deceptively, they end up paying three times what their budget started out to be by the time they finish. The slick GC knows this will happen long before they do and words the contract very shrewdly to make it easy for this to happen. We'll explore just how this can happen and it's much more subtle than you think. A homeowner with a burning desire to start a home improvement project with a very limited budget is a sitting duck for some sleight of hand maneuvers that will rope them in and drain their wallet by the time the project concludes.

Frankly, some homeowners should not even be *talking* to a General Contractor, they should be saving their money up while learning how to become their *own General Contractor.* That way, they can improve their home in incremental, manageable, affordable phases as their finances allow them to and their money will go much further.

Frankly, they don't even need me for this!

They just need some advice and direction so they can do it themselves and they would be *much better off* on so many levels. They can save money, have more control, protect themselves from fraud, do things on their own time and get exactly what they want. What's not to like about that?

Could I be any more honest and direct about this? You might wonder why I would work on a book which could conceivably eliminate potential clients for me. The reality is, if somebody can't really afford a GC, they won't be my clients anyway, but I would still like to help them out so they can handle it themselves successfully. Additionally, I want to help the people who really need to hire a GC and their better understanding of how to distinguish a good one from a real clown will protect them. The more they understand about the construction process, the more productively they can work with their GC and literally have more fun, which they should.

In short, my goal is to help *any* homeowner considering any project large or small to understand the techniques that a competent general contractor uses to achieve excellence and do it affordably. Specifically, we'll go over how to size up a project, prepare for it, manage it, hire the best subcontractors, keep it on schedule and deliver top quality workmanship and stay within your budget. These methods will be broken down in plain language that any homeowner can understand and they will equip them with a practical way to manage their own project from simply painting a window to a full scale new home construction. Homeowners will learn exactly what to do and what not to do, to create the right design, work with their local building and zoning department, evaluate and hire the best subcontractors, negotiate the contracts, save money and finish it on time.

So, let's get that started right now. Coffee break's over, it's time to punch in.

1   Should you trust a General Contractor?

Speaking as a General Contractor, no, you really shouldn't.

Can we agree that it's risky to enter into a business venture with someone and assume that the other party has your best interests in mind from start to finish? Caution is always necessary in any kind of situation where money changes hands. Hiring a GC is no different than hiring the right attorney or heart surgeon or auto mechanic in this respect. The right one will be an enormous help to you and the wrong one may create some costly damage.

General Contractors, or GC's have had a bad rap for years, making people wary. They should be. Honestly, it's deserved. If you pick 10 random people, it seems that 9 of them will have a personal story or know someone who has had a bad experience with a General Contractor. That's significant. There are too many people being take advantage of and having awful experiences out there, so if you can arm yourself with some basics of how things work, you can avoid some of the techniques which are used to separate people from their money and nothing more. Besides deceptive practices, there is the injustice of a job that is not well managed to the extent that it takes too long, involves too many mistakes, causes unnecessary stress on the client and does not conclude with pleasing results.

You are your best advocate to prevent this, but if you don't do this for a living, you are at a distinct disadvantage. Think you can spot all of the tricks because you're intelligent? I've see some very intelligent people by any standard get duped by some of the most amateur contractors more times than I can count. There is an inside game to this industry and if you are on the outside, you will be very vulnerable to its tactics. Do you think financial derivatives traders have a monopoly on sleight of hand techniques when it comes to complex transactions? Think again. People with doctorates and masters degrees get their pockets picked every day by guys who never finished high school, but own a general contracting company.

Even though the homeowner's counterproductive habits are to blame at times for some unpleasant experiences, there are enough legitimate examples of people getting ripped off by dishonest GC's to warrant their somewhat tainted reputation. The bad ones make it difficult for the rest of us, so frankly, the more homeowners arm themselves with the knowledge of how the process works, the less likely they will be taken advantage of. We'll cover some of the deceptive maneuvers that get used out there in subsequent chapters.

The dishonest GC's are often charming, personable, knowledgeable and excited to get something going for you. They seem to be good guys on the surface. Then the contract is signed, a deposit paid and the reality sinks in that you have just been hitched up for a ride you didn't want to take. They are never around, hard to reach, their subcontractors are not working in a disciplined, coordinated fashion and problems start to accumulate and often create a domino effect. There are unexpected huge price increases, quality issues, work stoppages, things verbally agreed to and promised just to pacify you for the moment...that never materialize. Disagreements, frustrations and anguish abound while the project never seems to end. It becomes like a slow motion train wreck, with a robbery slipped in, which unfolds over weeks or months.

Attempts to rectify issues with the GC are met with irritability, not cooperation and legitimate customer service. The project lingers on much longer than promised and there's always a lame excuse as to why. When the "virtual" conclusion to the project arrives, there's a long list of issues to be resolved and corrected after the work is supposedly complete and final payments requested. Sometimes, subcontractors don't get paid even though the homeowner pays the GC, who in turn, is supposed to pay the subcontractors. In reality, some GC's pocket the money and burn the subcontractor. How do you prevent that? We'll cover exactly how, later in the book.

These reasons and many others make some people wary of GC's and frankly, they should be. The reality is, there are plenty of guys out there who are not capable of doing anything more than ripping people off. I know. I've cleaned up plenty of the messes they've left behind. You wonder how they get another client and the reality is, many people simply put up with them because their neighbor or acquaintance did and it's too embarrassing to admit you're getting jerked around. It's much more satisfying to brag about the huge addition that you're putting on your house while you're lacing up your golf shoes at the club. Nobody ever wants to stand in the middle of the locker room at the club and declare:

"Hey everyone, I just want to announce that I did something really ill-advised recently. I signed a contract with a guy I hardly knew and didn't take the time to research his credentials. Now he's really getting the best of me because I'm not quite sure how this whole renovation thing works anyway and it's already costing me 40% more than I expected. I sure wish I wasn't such a sucker! Now, who wants to go play 18 holes with me?"

This speech will never happen in the middle of a locker room. The same country club member who is getting ripped off wants to sell you some life insurance or be your financial planner, your CPA or remove your gall bladder. They are professionals there to have fun and network their businesses and services and nobody wants to come across as a fool in this context. It could cost them some business. Many, not all, but many of these people will suffer silently and privately regret what they got themselves into. They'll just survive it, then finally, when the project is done, focus on enjoying it as best they can. Nobody will know the truth about the knucklehead GC they hired and friends who stop by will simply see the end results of the ordeal.

They might even become envious and *insist* on getting the name of the GC who was used because they want something similar done to their house. And so...the cycle continues on with the next victim...

At this point, you should know some important things about the way I approach being a General Contractor. First off, I have been paid 100% in full by every client for every sized project I have ever managed in my whole life. This is the gold standard test as to their satisfaction with the work: They paid in full. I have also *never* had a subcontractor file a lien on any project which I have managed ever in my life. This is the gold standard test that they were also paid 100% in full on all of my projects. To date, I have not met a single GC yet, who can say this about their career. It's that rare. It really shouldn't be the case, but it is and that's a shame.

It's just good business to do quality work in an honest fashion. You earn your future clients by taking care of your present clients. Beyond that, when you treat your subcontractors more like business partners and keep their best interests in mind, they look out for your best interests too, which means they always make sure they do quality work for your clients. They know a good GC makes their job a lot easier and they can sleep well knowing they will be paid. You earn that with them and they pay you back with better prices, better workmanship and consistent reliability. It just pays to be a good, honest GC if you're going to be one at all.

That being said, it seems as though the soft economy in recent years has brought forth an influx of fraudulent behavior as small construction and remodeling companies everywhere scramble to survive. I've seen too many situations where General Contractors are not paying their bills and often when that happens, some good honest subcontractors suffer unfairly. Liens get filed, people lawyer up and everyone loses money and time. It can be a jungle out there if you link up with the wrong General Contractor. How do you know they paid the subcontractors? We'll cover that very important question later on in more detail, but he short answer is, you don't rely on their honesty, you pay the subcontractors yourself.

That's why so many people would be much better off to simply be their *own* General Contractor. You know where the money is, you know what everything costs to the penny, you know where the subcontractors are, you control the pace of the project. You get exactly what you want and you don't have to deal with the somewhat murky prospect of working with a GC. In my opinion, the need for certain homeowners to become their own General Contractors has never been greater. Now more than ever, people need to protect their homes, be cautious about who they hand money over to and try to make every spare nickel they spend deliver the impact of a dollar. Frankly, this is not beyond reach, with the right knowledge.

This may seem like a daunting task to some. Hey, are you a parent? THAT's a daunting task. Being a GC is *much* easier. However, parenting skills will come in very handy in the process. Somebody has to be the adult, the one in charge. Somebody has to explain the expectations and lead the way and watch the progress and encourage good behavior and address any unacceptable behavior. There will be some Fridays where everyone deserves some cake. Yeah cake! There will be some Mondays where somebody needs a time out.

If you're just an average parent, you already have the core skills of a phenomenal GC.

2   What does a competent GC do and why should I think like one?

If you can look at a project from the perspective of a competent GC, you will be able to think more practically and strategically about any improvements you would like to make to your home. A good GC is constantly considering what needs to be done to achieve the goal measured against time, budget, sequencing, quality control, safety, weather, lead time and practicality.

The responsibilities of a good GC include, but are not limited to:

Clarification of the goals of the project

Confirming with the local building and zoning department that the scope of work which is intended to be done can be done without any violations or restrictions imposed by the local building and zoning laws

Committing the goals to a clearly written document form, whether it be architectural drawings or written bullet points or both

Assembling the right group of subcontractors to handle each element of the project and communicating the project goals to them one by one using the written goals and drawings

Meeting the subcontractors on the site for clarification and opportunities for questions in order for them to create their written bids for the project

Collecting their written bids and studying them over for accuracy and completeness and communicating any errors or omissions to them in order for them to make any necessary revisions

Moving this bid information to a spreadsheet which is constantly updated and totaled as new bids are received, providing more and more total cost information as the days go by

Reviewing the information periodically with the homeowner to assess the intended budget versus the actual bids, assess the estimated time needed for completion for each subcontractor, consider any issues that were unforeseen and generally observe how the project is shaping up logistically and financially

Finalizing the necessary bids to accomplish the project with an effort made to achieve a known cost for each line item on the spreadsheet and eliminating all or as many undetermined cost line item issues as possible

Creating the construction contract using the spreadsheet to determine the overall total cost and describing the scope of work and a realistic target completion date

Providing warranty details on the quality of the workmanship

Working with the local building and zoning department to fill out the construction permit application and getting the necessary permit fees paid

Making sure the work site is properly prepared to start work to the extent that the local building and zoning department guidelines are met and permit properly posted on the site

Contacting the subcontractors and getting them started, managing their individual efforts in terms of quality, timing and payments and confirming that they are properly insured

Communicating with any suppliers and coordinating their efforts based on their interaction with the client. For example, meeting with the cabinetry company and the homeowner to design the cabinetry, or finalizing the granite counter top material selection and coordinating it's purchase from the supplier where the homeowner selected it, then making sure the fabricator picks it up and measures the cabinetry on the work site prior to installation

Managing any changes whatsoever that occur in the scope of work during the project with clearly written, signed documents called "change orders"

Keeping the home owner informed and asking for their decisions on any line items not already confirmed in an orderly way, anticipating when the decision will be needed in the sequence of the project and communicating well in advance of those dates in the timeline

Coordinating the incremental payments for all of the subcontractors commensurate with the work they have accomplished to date and making any deposits necessary on items to be ordered

Tracking every penny on a spreadsheet called a "draw statement," which is a snapshot of all line items and what has been paid so far and how much remains to be paid for each line

Always looking for an opportunity to save money on any line item as new information becomes available, changes are made, or market conditions change

Periodically helping each subcontractor do their job in any way necessary to keep the momentum of the project going forward

Making sure the inspections necessary by the local building and zoning department are all scheduled and successfully passed so that the work can continue to the next phase

Constantly making lists and updating them on what remains to be done for completion until the list is blank

You might say this is just a brief overview. This is by no means an exhaustive list, but you get the general idea. Frankly, before I make the job sound overly complex, I should also humbly point out that the most important tool I personally use most often is a shop vac or a broom. Seriously.

Toward the end of a project, as the hardwood floors are freshly finished, the walls are crisply painted, the cabinetry is firmly in place and the marble tile is gleaming, there are always few issues that the homeowner brings up at the 11th hour. They want to replace one more vanity, add one more power outlet, replace one more toilet, a window, you get the idea...and now you have to work around not damaging your recently completed, pristine workmanship. So, as we carefully cut into a wall, pry off some window casing, unbolt a toilet and concentrate on not damaging anything in the process, there I am, shop vac in one hand, clean rag in the other, hoping to protect the finishes as we perform the final surgical maneuvers. You put down drop cloths, but after the drop cloths are tossed into the back of a van a few dozen times, they really don't provide anything but superficial protection. Light powder from drywall dust gets embedded into the drop cloths meaning that you really need to clean up behind every subcontractor until the last one leaves. This is not very glamorous, but it's an essential part of finishing the job.

Should they clean up after themselves? Sure. Do they, to the extent you need them to? I'll let you decide. As for me, I'll keep my shop vac handy with a stack of clean microfiber rags...I have to make sure everything is spotless, as it should be and I am the final inspector on every job. Is that exciting or fun? Not really. But, you want to make sure everything looks spectacular at the end because even if you do everything right, but the plumber smudges a dirty work boot on the new master bathroom floor tile and leaves a mark, the homeowner will see that and be upset and fixate on that. They just spent an enormous amount of money, so they want everything done right--and they deserve that.

As an aside, I once had a conversation with a gentleman who managed a very elegant 5 star restaurant. I was asking him about the rigorous journey of how he achieved such a milestone and he said it certainly wasn't easy, which made perfect sense to me. Then he explained that the difference between a 4 star and a 5 star restaurant could be as simple as a single, tiny water spot found on a single piece of silverware. That made an impression on me. A good GC makes sure all of the little things are covered, however menial they may be.

Why should you think like a GC? By understanding realistically what a good one does, you can take on that role. For example, by knowing that you will have to read over the bids for accuracy, which is not guaranteed, you will understand that mistakes can happen and you have to keep checking for them before you move forward with any contractual agreements. If you are unfamiliar with how to read a subcontractor's bid over, then have the subcontractor explain it to you line by line. It should not be hard to understand. It should be very straightforward, so if you have questions, don't feel foolish, you may have uncovered a legitimate, foolish error. Reading bids is like riding a bike, so once you get the feel for what a bid looks like, the next bid will be easier to comprehend. The bottom line is that you are constantly checking and re-checking for quality and accuracy in every detail of the project and by taking on that mindset, you will hone your ability to spot an error long before it ever becomes a real problem.

A practical GC skill involves the ability to ask questions of anyone in a friendly way which promotes communication. There are always issues which need more clarity and if you ask anyone with a sincere and respectful tone, you will usually get some very useful help in return. A good GC makes an effort to connect with everyone who can participate in accomplishing the goals of the project, no matter how small their individual role is. If you can communicate effectively, this may be the most important skill you can possess to Think like a General Contractor.

Let me give you an example of how good communication will save you money and help you take care of your home more effectively. Here's realistic scenario. Let's say you have a problem and you think you need a repairman out to your house to fix it, which will cost some money. Here is a strategy that I want you to pay close attention to and apply it to any circumstances which you find yourself in where you think you might need to pay someone to come out to your house to fix something.

Let's say your air conditioner isn't cooling your home properly. Are you an expert in air conditioning? Not likely. It will help immensely for you to get an HVAC (Heating, Ventilation and Air Conditioning) company on the phone and to be honest, polite and respectful while asking some very simple questions. You could make it clear that you're not satisfied with the way the system is cooling and ask if they could help you diagnose the problem a bit over the phone first before you incurred the expense of a service call. Make it clear that you would simply like to save you both some time and money and hassle. That's reasonable.

A reputable HVAC company will respond to you very willingly for this simple request. You see, they don't make very much money to send someone out to fix a simple problem like adjusting the digital thermostat properly, if it's as simple as that, so they don't want to waste their time on trivial things either. You are actually helping them out by offering to maneuver around your house while on your cell phone and to try a few simple potential solutions first. This is a win-win. Note that the person who answers the phone may not be the one who can help you. If that's the case, ask to talk to the owner or a service technician. They may need to call you back. While you wait for that call, you could certainly call another HVAC company up as well to move things along faster.

Do you know it could be as simple as moving a couch away from a floor vent or closing and latching a window or pulling a curtain closed or even changing a filthy furnace filter? Let the expert walk you through some issues to check and all the while, you will get a valuable air conditioning system education on the phone. This is a cost free way of possibly finding the issue and correcting it without any service call.

If the problem persists, you will have the peace of mind that you legitimately tried everything first before incurring the service charge. Therefore, it's OK for them to take over at this point and solve the problem with their expertise by sending the technician to your home. You will hang up the phone knowing more about your AC system than when you started.

If the technician has to come out, you will learn even more if you make the time to follow them around to diagnose the problem. All the while, you can ask questions (politely, with consideration for their time and showing them respect) and offer to hold a flashlight for them as they examine sections of your system. This simple act of being helpful to them will come in handy whenever you need to hire any expert to work on your home. Hold the flashlight, as in hold *your* flashlight. Have a good one handy for this purpose always ready to go with fresh batteries. Ask questions about everything they do. Simple enough? You cannot imagine how much you will learn by simply talking to someone like this while being helpful to them. It's like having a university professor come into your basement and personally teach you the course in their respective field of expertise in a relaxed, conversational manner. It's your air conditioner after all, wouldn't you like to know more about how it works and how to take care of it? You can either read the manual if you can find it, or have a conversation with a human being. I prefer the latter...

In the early Fall, have a reputable HVAC company (we'll cover more on exactly how to choose great contractors later...) come out to clean your furnace. They often have "specials" for $50-$75 to do this and it's an important maintenance issue to get in the habit of each year. They can service your air conditioner in the late spring as part of a package deal. Have this done, it's money well spent. They will clean debris out of your exterior AC compressor unit and check your coolant pressure to detect any leaks or low levels and recharge if necessary. This is all important to do to keep your AC and furnace running smoothly for years to come--which saves money. An AC system low on coolant will run longer to cool your house and use more electricity and be harder on the system than one with adequate coolant. Watch what they do and ask them about each part they are focusing on and always ask them what their advice would be for any matters concerning the long term health of your equipment. Talk, listen, learn. This may sound like common sense, but most people don't consider capturing this free educational moment. They open the door, let the guy in, ask how much it will be when he's done and write a check. What a wasted opportunity...

You can use this strategy with any potential repair work that you face. Always insist on trying things first over the phone by making the point that you don't want to waste your time or their time if you can solve the problem with a few simple issues to check first.

That being said, I would add that I always carry four items with me at all times as a General Contractor. You don't have to personally carry them around, as I do, but if you are trying to solve a problem knowing where you can quickly find these four things will be very helpful. They are:

1. A powerful, very compact flashlight (mine uses just one AA battery)

2. A small, pocket sized pad and pen

3. A smart phone with a camera

4. A tape measure

You can solve just about any mystery with these four tools and make the appropriate game plan. Your trouble shooting phone conversations may lead to the need to write down an additional phone number or name, or even an email address or website address so have a pen and pad in your back pocket. Even in the daylight hours, you may need to examine something in the basement or under a sink without adequate lighting, so have that flashlight ready. Some easily clip on your belt. You also may need to convey something to the person on the phone by taking a picture of it and emailing it to them (from your phone) while speaking to them. This is a skill you should have if you don't know how to do that. It comes in very handy for a situation like this. When you show an expert who you are consulting with on the phone a clear picture of what you're looking at, it's like they are right there with you-- instantly. You can imagine, it speeds up everything, which is very useful.

Smart phones are becoming so much easier to use and so much more powerful and useful, it's money well spent to have one. It will save you enormous amounts of time and money. Having the internet handy at your fingertips to look up information on any questions which arise is extremely useful. The cameras on smart phones are phenomenal today as well.

I've snapped pictures of serial numbers, broken pipe issues, carpentry measurement questions, floor tile grout colors, shower head styles, door hinge finishes, cabinet dimensions you name it! You cannot fathom how valuable digital picture technology is when you need to solve something quickly and accurately. I can communicate with an architect from a supplier's showroom and email a picture of an item which I have a question on and he can open it in his smart phone wherever he is and we can get the matter settled and solved in seconds, not days. I can communicate this way with clients as well. One client of mine traveled all over the world for his job while we worked on his house and he was always in the loop opening pictures of important issues on his smart phone in every country he woke up in each morning. It's like he was there each day even though he was often on the other side of the world, literally.

I realize many of you already have a great smart phone and this advice seems pretty elementary. On the other hand, are you starting to realize you're much more prepared to do this than you thought? I hope so. Many of the skills you already have will be harnessed to save you money and to achieve excellence in your project, no matter your budget. By the time you take good care of your house for a while and have enough educational conversations with experts, you will have built up a familiarity of some important concepts that will help you when you do have the need to tackle a project of more serious magnitude.

Do you have aspirations about doing something that will cost more than you can currently afford? That's fine. Start gradually educating yourself on all aspects of your home in the meantime and by doing so, you are preparing yourself to be your own GC further down the road. Learn from the experts you interact with in the process of caring for your house and get to know a little more every chance you have about every major system in your house. You don't have to give up months of your life studying courses on construction management at the local college to gain a practical understanding, it can happen in small, manageable bites over time if you seize the moments as they unfold.

A good GC is always learning, always discussing the particulars of even the most routine tasks while constantly looking for ways to do things better, more efficiently, more easily and more affordably. Homeowners could benefit immensely from this mindset .

3   How much do things really cost?

This is such an important issue, it merits getting into as early as possible. Where there is certainly a bit of a disparity of what things cost in different regions of the US, you will be smart to ponder the following realistic price ranges for the types of projects you want to tackle. By having a realistic range in mind, you can at least plan financially for the work you want to get done some day and not be shocked when you start the process with some unrealistic number in mind. So let's dig right in.

Let's start with the kitchen. My price perspective is based on the Chicago, Illinois metropolitan area. If you are in a rural part of the US, you can likely do things a bit cheaper, if you are in some major metro areas on the east coast or west coast, you may have to pay a little more, so make those mental adjustments depending on your circumstances.

You have to ask yourself what your real intentions are, especially with the kitchen. If your intentions are to generate a very indisputable "WOW" when your guests walk in, this will point you in a more expensive direction. You'll want to address everything from the floors to the ceiling and at least consider the windows with respect to their size and location. This means layout, walls, appliances, custom cabinets, natural stone countertops and much more. The more WOW, the more money. Anyone who tries to imply that you can get WOW results on a tiny budget is usually trying to sell you something pretty cheesy, so beware of the "bargain" kitchen makeover specialists out there.

Now, your intentions may be to simply have a functional kitchen with some cabinets and countertops that don't scream "1971!" That is a noble goal and considerably less money to execute than upgrading a kitchen in a neighborhood lined with $5 million homes. If you can live with your floors, ceiling, windows and current appliances, you will save a lot of money and likely be able to make do without the premium expense of custom cabinets. The big box hardware stores have plenty of choices that will likely work for you and your wallet will truly appreciate that route. If you're really working with a rough kitchen to start with, just doing this will create a dramatic, significant difference.

If you really wanted to do a floor to ceiling "high end" kitchen makeover, you will spend plus or minus $100,000. This sometimes shocks people, who live in a very, very nice house and just received a $35,000 quarterly bonus at work and want to renovate their kitchen. I get these calls all the time. They usually know what they want and have a picture from a magazine cover to show me. This is useful, for capturing the visual of what they want, but it also triggers a real sense of disbelief when they find out the price of "beautiful." They are so often *stunned.*

The appliances alone could easily exceed $25,000 if you go with some premium brand name ovens, refrigerators, dishwashers (by the way, many high end kitchens have 2 dishwashers...), wine coolers, microwaves, exhaust fans and refrigerated island drawers. Just the natural stone counter tops could exceed $8,000 and if you choose high end plumbing fixtures, your 2 sinks and your pot filler at the stove, you're over your $35,000 budget before we pay anyone to install anything or get a building permit. Poof...goes your quarterly bonus...

Notice there are not cabinets, floors, plumber charges, electrician charges, building permits, windows, drywall work, raised ceiling work, natural stone backsplash installation, painting, carpentry charges and lighting fixture charges included yet? There's your $65,000 in other invoices. Can you see how this can go past $100,000 very quickly?

You can easily ratchet that down and save money by not going with high end custom cabinets, but visiting a big box hardware store and working with their kitchen department. If you choose their standard sized cabinets, go with overlay cabinet doors, choose among their standard paint and stain colors and have them install them for you, you will save a substantial amount of money. Just by going this route, you could save literally 65% of the cost of your cabinets alone vs. custom made cabinets. Sound good? You can hold off on doing the floors if they look good enough now, choose a cultured or engineered (both terms mean man-made) counter top material, select reasonably priced light and plumbing fixtures and choose quality, but not the top of the line appliances, paint the kitchen yourself and manage the job yourself and make your kitchen look extremely beautiful for more like $35,000.

Do you see where this is going when you have the skills to manage the job yourself? If you don't know the difference between overlay and inset cabinets, chances are you would be just as happy going this route. Overlay cabinet doors close against the face frame and are the most common style you will see. You may even have that style already. Inset cabinet doors close into and flush with the face frames and are considered more elegant and prestigious. They are also considerably more expensive. If you don't know the difference, chances are you are not that particular about it. Why pay a premium for something that does not matter to you in the scheme of things? It's similar to why spend more than $5 on cabernet when you can't tell the difference between that and $250 cabernet. To others, it would be inconceivable to sip anything less than $250 cabernet. You decide what's important and if you want to pay the premiums involved with each level of refinement--in any project you tackle. Study custom cabinetry, then study the cabinetry in the big box hardware stores and decide which represents the route you prefer to take. There are trade-offs, but some are actually worth it and only you can decide. There is no shame in going to the big box store for your cabinets, if that is your budget range. You can make it work and get some beautiful results.

Let's talk about bathrooms. If you want a high end master bathroom renovation, there are some areas where your decisions will affect which direction the total costs end up in a dramatic way. The typical upscale renovation starts at about $24,000 (without a new tub) and can go way past that (with a new tub) in a hurry. If you insist on natural stone material like marble, you can add to that. If you can make the time to find a nice looking porcelain tile, you would be better off. This is less expensive material and is cheaper and easier to take care of year after year. Natural stone can stain much easier and has to be sealed periodically. Porcelain is much more durable and forgiving and wipes up more easily. You'll need to seal the grout, but you don't have to seal all porcelain tile. Always check with the supplier to confirm this. Just choosing porcelain over natural stone will save thousands by the time you consider your floor, your shower (floor, walls, possibly ceiling) and any backsplash features that involve tile. When you consider how much effort you want to put into caring for the tile, or pay someone to do it, you may not want natural stone as a material. It's beautiful, but has some on-going responsibilities to consider. Again, you know who you are and the caliber of home you have and your budget. Let that guide you accordingly.

As a quick aside, an upscale car dealer once told me he always has a steady low mileage, used sports car supply created by men in their 50's and 60's who thought they really wanted one until driving them day in and day out wreaked havoc on any existing lower back problems. The stiff suspensions and low seats made it hard to maneuver and twist to enter and exit the cars. They often traded them in a few months after they bought them, in agony, with low miles on the odometer. The moral: Choose carefully, as you may not want to accept the hassles or costs of caring for natural stone materials even if you *had to have it*... If, however, that is the look and feel you want, there is really no substitute for natural stone. You decide.

If you start changing the layout of the bathroom and moving the location of the shower, tub and toilet and such, expect to get an $8,000 bill or more from the plumber and the carpenters will do a couple thousand dollars of extra work tearing floors and walls apart for that to happen. An HVAC expert will get busy re-routing some heating and cooling ducts and the carpenters will have to close it all up behind them at the end. If you can keep everything (toilet, shower, sinks, tub) in its original position and simply upgrade the fixtures, you may have a $700 bill from the plumber. Can you see the significant differences in costs for the different scenarios?

You can get a new tub for your master bathroom, but very few people actually use them more than once or twice a year. Some hate to clean them. Mostly, they like the look of a tub and the ambiance of having the "luxury" of a tub, but rarely use them. Simple "upscale" soaker tubs can cost $2000. Air jet tubs start around $4,000. A big box store carries generic, no frills tubs starting at $125 or less if you can live with plastic. Don't think you're harming yourself on resale value for your home if you avoid having a fancy tub in the master bathroom. I have yet to hear a story of somebody not buying a house because it lacked a tub. If it was an important issue to a buyer, these days the buyer would make an offer and demand a tub to be installed as well. Enough said.

Your vanity cabinet could either be custom made, a big box hardware store model or an old piece of furniture retro fitted to accept plumbing fixtures. Or, you might go with something even simpler--a pedestal sink or sinks, without a cabinet at all. All of these have price ramifications so think about how you want your bathroom to look, consult an architect if you are wanting to change the floor plan of the bathroom and brace yourself for the costs to be incurred if you have to change the floor plan. Many older homes have tiny master bathrooms, so it's popular to expand them and change the configuration of where everything lays out. The more fixtures you can keep in their current positions, the cheaper it will be to do.

Heated floors (electric) are a very nice touch and can start at about $1,400. A steam shower unit can run $2,750. A nice new toilet can start at $90 from a hardware store and quickly jump to $250 for a "brand name" toilet with some panache. You decide what look you have to have and make that call.

The ceiling can be a 2-$3,000 if you raise it and create a tray ceiling or a vaulted ceiling with bead board and faux beams for a vintage, country look. Wood paneled wainscoting can be a $1500 and up. Tiled wainscoting could be more.

If you want a simple bathroom makeover and more budget minded selections are appropriate for your home and you manage the job yourself, you can do some wonderful things for just $2,000. This can include a new vanity, sink, toilet, new tiled floor and a nice paint job. Shop the big box stores and consider painting everything yourself at the end, it's an even greater savings to do that. Paint is the least expensive, highest impact return on investment you can find. Plus, you can tackle it on a weekend or at night at your leisure. If you haven't already, learn to paint. Practice in a closet if you have to, but you will be glad you did. One more thing about paint: Buy the best paint you can find. It is always cheaper to buy the best paint you can find and more expensive to buy the cheapest paint. Counterintuitive, right? Premium quality paint covers in fewer coats, so you buy less, lasts longer, so you don't have to paint as often, cleans up better and looks better, much, much longer. Always buy the good stuff. Enough said.

What if you have a basement which has concrete foundation walls, a concrete foundation floor and some steel columns holding up some steel beams, with exposed floor joists throughout? This is the blank canvas for a myriad of things to do with a myriad of price points. Let's start at the bottom. If you simply dry walled the walls and ceiling and had some recessed can lights in the ceiling and the proper amount of power outlets (per code) in the walls, carpeted the floor and had some internet and cable TV jacks installed, you could do this for about $12,000 plus or minus in a modest sized home. This creates an immediately useful room for kids to play and gives you a platform to build upon for the future. You can add a built in entertainment center, a bar, an exercise area or separate exercise room altogether. You can add closets, storage areas, hobby rooms, extra shelving and so on. You can have a netted golf swing area, a home theater, an office, you name it. The basement can be your least expensive "instant" addition if it is currently unfinished.

Some people have the basement finished just as nice as any area of the house with top notch molding and engineered wood flooring. Note that potential flooding requires the use of man-made flooring systems in the basement which can withstand water damage and not expand as regular hardwood flooring would in a flood. Using real hardwood in a basement is an expensive mistake in a flood as real hardwood will absorb and expand when soaked in water and will expand with powerful, damaging force which can burst through 2x4 walls and even crack foundation walls. The good news is there are products which have the look of real hardwood (some actually are real hardwood surfaces for the top 1/8 of an inch laminated to an engineered base) mounted on a strip of heated, pressed glue and wood products which is much more stable and will not expand in a flood. You see the nice surface, but below the surface is a sophisticated subfloor designed to not absorb water in the event of a flood.

Speaking of floods, it is just good common sense to make sure your basement does not have any water seepage issues before investing in any upgrades and address them first. Even a dry basement can conceivably flood without protection from its sump pump. The sump pump essentially rids the basement of all the water which is captured by the buried pipes (drain tile) which run along the (exterior or interior or both) of the perimeter of the foundation walls. These pipes generally form a continuous loop which starts and ends in the sump pit. The pit fills with the water which drains into it from the drain tile pipes outside and the sump pump is eventually triggered to activate at a certain water level and it discharges the water up and out of the basement to the exterior of the house at ground level. Some sump pumps carry the water to a village storm water system. Either way, this is a critically important function, but eventually, all sump pumps fail, so we always recommend installing a battery operated back-up sump pump system. These are constantly charged and ready to go in the event of a primary mechanical sump pump failure or a power failure--each of which can lead to a flood is the drain tile fills the sump pit and it starts to overflow into your basement. Good reliable systems like this start at about $1700 installed. You should have one if you don't already. GC's are always thinking ahead about how to protect things and you should too. Do you have car insurance? You get the idea. If you paid for it, protect it.

If you are having issues with water seeping into your basement through the seam where the wall meets the floor, then this could indicate an issue with your exterior drain tile or lack thereof, not effectively capturing and re-routing the ground water to the sump pit. In a worst case scenario, you will need exterior or interior drain tile installed. Interior drain tile is literally installed by cutting into the concrete floor and digging a trench around the inside perimeter of your basement. It is then buried in gravel, topped with cement and the tile terminates in your sump pit. This is the worst case scenario if this needs to be done as it is messy and will cost some money to accomplish. However, your seepage problem could also be caused by something much less expensive and invasive to fix as well, so you need to call in some experts to investigate.

Look into some reputable water proofing companies to visit your home personally before going any further with any plans to finish your basement. Have conversations with several and look for consistencies in their speculations about what is causing the seepage. Take pictures, email them. Discuss them. If you have any vertical foundation wall cracks that are oozing moisture over time, there are some effective ways to repair these with liquid crack filler products which can be strategically injected. Consult the water proofing companies and listen to their suggested courses of action. After asking some reliable sources for some companies they recommend (neighbors, friends, local building and zoning department) pick the one who guarantees their work in writing and has some references with similar cracks that you can check.

Sometimes, the problem is simple and requires some minor landscaping adjustments so that rain water can pitch away from the foundation properly and not collect and percolate down the side of your foundation wall and overwhelm the drain tile. Other times, placing a downspout in a different location will eliminate a seepage problem. Always study what the conditions are right above where the water is seeping in at ground level outside and look for puddles, soil that appears to pitch back toward the house and gutter and downspout effectiveness near the area.

I finished a basement once with 2 fireplaces, a bedroom, a bathroom, a powder room, a billiard room, a wine cellar, a bar area, a home theater and a card room. It was well protected by 2 sump pumps in two separate sump pits and 2 battery back-up sump pumps. Beyond that, we wired up a separate electrical panel for a natural gas powered generator outside in the event there was a prolonged power outage. That way, if the homeowner was out of town, all of the important circuits (furnaces, garage doors, sump pumps, refrigerators, the office, the security system) would have uninterrupted power in the event of an outage. You get the idea--always think ahead when it comes to the basement if you choose to invest money in finishing it.

How about a nice addition for a sun room or a library or an office or a family room? You can expect to pay in the $60,000 range for even a modest addition if you want a 12 x 12 room bump out into the back yard. Just digging the dirt for the foundation, assuming it's as deep as your full depth foundation could run you $7,000. The concrete could cost $11,000. The lumber could easily run over $10,000. You may have to move some underground utilities--add a few thousand for that. You may need to install a new electric meter as you will remove your old one and relocate the new one on the new addition or somewhere else--add a few grand. Framing labor could be $6,000. Lumber and siding could easily run $8,000. The drywall could be $3,000. Simple asphalt roofing, aluminum gutters, soffits and fascia could be $3,500. Can you see how quickly things add up? Don't forget the fact that your existing basement will open up into your new addition basement, so have the existing basement wall saw cut will run at least $1,400. The windows could easily run $8,000. There will be choices to make for siding, with brick costing more than lap board and shingle somewhere in between. The inside of the addition could easily involve an additional $10,000 if you had a talented trim carpenter finish it in cherry wood with some built in shelves and double French doors and a box beam ceiling. Can you get the idea where this could go if it was larger than 12 x 12 or if you added a bathroom to the addition? Add a wood-burning fireplace with a full masonry chimney and you could add $11,000 to the total. If you went with a vent-less gas fireplace, you could reduce this to $5,000 and still have a nice brick or natural stone surround and hearth.

Just adding a simple powder room on to this addition could add $12,000 for even a basic essentials scenario and anything more elaborate would be more still.

Here is an important side note to adding more bathrooms, or a second laundry room to your house. Your local building and zoning department may calculate that your current individual water service supply line which connects your house to the city's main water supply (usually underneath or alongside your street) is insufficient. The current number of fixtures in your house may be adequately served, but if you increase that number of fixtures, it may exceed the accepted total demand for your current water supply line size. In other words, if you add another bathroom, you could exceed the code for your current sized water supply line and it would require digging up your old line and replacing it with a new, larger line.

For example, you may have a one inch supply line now and be required to go to an inch and quarter line because there are now more fixtures (because of the bathroom addition or second laundry room added) demanding water from your line's ability to serve them all adequately. This can be a costly thing (possibly $6,000 or more) to find out about before you are too far into the design process, which is another reason to discuss your intentions with the city. You want to know exactly what you are in for before you start planning any improvements so you know how to budget properly. A good GC likes to eliminate surprises of any kind. Finding out you need a new water line to accommodate your plans would be a costly surprise.

When it comes to costs, as a general rule, the smaller the addition, the more costly it is in terms of cost per square foot. The enormous cost of excavation and concrete take up a higher percentage of the project in a smaller addition and skew the project toward a higher cost per square foot. In a typical two story home, there are plenty of less expensive materials like framing lumber to offset the higher cost of excavation and concrete to minimize their expensive impact on the project and result in a lower cost per square foot as a result. That's why, it is generally cheaper to build "up," rather than "out" when doing an addition, because you can avoid the excavation and concrete.

Let's take that same 12 x 12 room and make it a playroom over the existing garage. Your cost would be more like $40,000 right off the bat and if you reduced the number of windows in this scenario, it could easily move closer to $35,000.

Can you see the cost advantage now? Anytime you can avoid digging, you can avoid a whole series of additional costs to contend with. Many people bought a ranch house when they were first married and after a few children, it becomes a bit cramped. The family room used to be where Mom and Dad relaxed, watched TV, read books and talked. Now, it's a congested intersection of video games, toys, the expected innocent and loud commotion of children having fun, conflicts over what should be on TV and plenty of other things that squeeze the tranquility out of the room for Mom and Dad. They long for a little separation from their energetic children and we always suggest looking to finish the basement first and foremost (if it's not finished) for their new playroom. If they need the whole basement for storage and finishing it is not practical, we suggest building "up" rather than "out" for the cost savings. It just makes sense. Thinking like a GC means looking for ways to do things in a practical, cost efficient manner at all times. This is the sure route to adding value and comfort to your home.

These costs are obviously general idea costs. Let's face it. We live in a world where we can spend $250 on new a simple gas stove with an oven that can easily bake cookies while heating up a can of soup. We can also spend $14,000 on a new gas stove with an oven that can easily bake cookies while heating up a can of soup. In some houses, it would literally be inappropriate to install anything less than a $14,000 oven/stove. Only you know who you are and what is appropriate for your house. I like to tell people that (as of today) a 2 x 4 costs about $2 and it costs the same whether we install it in a $125,000 house or a $4,000,000 house. So, it's not the basic materials which create the huge price disparities among houses, it's the caliber of finishes, appliances, fixtures, cabinetry, tile and other assorted features which drive the costs up or down. Brick or natural stone siding will cost more than traditional wood siding and a slate roof can nearly double the cost of a cedar shake roof. Copper gutters can double the cost of aluminum gutters. That's why it's very tricky question to ask how much it will cost to build a house per square foot. When asked that question, I always answer with another question: "What do you want in it? What do you want on it?" I can show the cost per square foot of previous projects and use them as examples of finishes to start from, but it's difficult to blurt out a cost per square foot number without knowing the caliber of finishes someone expects until they actually choose them. There are plenty of slick GC's out there who will blurt out any number that sounds attractive to a potential client, sign them to a contract, then shower them with cost increases as the project continues. We'll talk more about that in more detail later in the book.

Speaking of costs, let's talk about a few more practical ways to control costs. Your light fixtures and plumbing fixtures can have an alarming range of prices for seemingly similar products. This is worth noting. There are some enormous premiums paid every day for certain brand name plumbing fixtures which carry a certain perceived level of quality and make all of the desired statements of class and sophistication about their consumers. If you live and die by this, by all means, open your wallet wide and keep moving the decimal point to the right. You have to live with it each day so if certain fixtures captivate you and their price tags are not an issue, have at it. Your home and its components are a very personalized configuration of your unique tastes and if you have to have something, there is your answer.

On the other hand, all of my clients, regardless of their net worth, had one thing in common: A very burning desire to reduce costs and maximize value, so that is the world I live in. In that world of frugality, the internet is your friend. You can find all sorts of discount plumbing fixture operations who have business models geared toward creating bargains to entice you. Seize the moment and take advantage of those bargains if you find things that suit you. As the consumer, you have enormous leverage these days and there are companies working around the clock to figure out ways to save you money by offering discontinued products, off brand products and things that plain and simple did not sell well through the traditional distribution channels. There are too many bargains out there to pass up.

Know this, you might even achieve a further discount if you buy your plumbing fixtures over the internet, but through the plumbing company that you will have install them. Or, you can test the waters by saying you are in effect, a General Contractor and curious about any "contractor pricing" offered. You may be surprised, some internet based retailers will discount their already aggressive prices even further. Always ask. Now, to be up front, if you buy your plumbing fixtures directly yourself and the plumber installs them, you will not be protected by the plumber's warranty if they fail and need to be replaced or repaired.

A plumber will typically warranty a fixture for a year and replace it or fix it if it fails inside that time frame. The way they protect their risk from this potential cost is by purchasing the fixture for you at a contractor discount and selling it to you on a cost plus profit basis. That $250 toilet may have cost the plumber $200. He buys it, sells it to you and keeps the $50 profit on that item for taking the risk he may need to repair it someday in the next year. You will certainly pay him a labor charge on top of that fixture charge to install it too, mind you. You can imagine if you need $25,000 worth of fixtures, there could be $5,000 or more in profit to the plumber on just the fixtures alone if he buys them for you. Some people would rather take that risk themselves and save the $5,000. Just so you know, the internet can save you money, but you need to consider the ramifications of warranty with your plumber. There are situations where this risk is advisable to take and others where it is better to keep the plumber's warranty at least through the first year. You should think it through to consider when you are the most comfortable to assume any risks.

The same scenario holds true for light fixtures. You can see some amazing items on line. There are some instances where you will pay $250 for a sconce light at a retail brick and mortar store that you can find for $35 on an internet site. Now, there are some risks that you take when items are shipped, making sure they arrive intact, but you can see the potential savings that can be achieved if you are so inclined to search the internet.

I knew a homeowner with a beautiful, $1,000,000+ house adorned with lovely lantern style lights at every exterior door and flanking all three garage doors. They were stunning and looked very elegant and expensive. She only paid $10 a piece at an internet store. Shop for bargains---they're out there!

If you are not comfortable with not physically the item before you purchase it, then look for a nearby retail store which specializes in selling overstocked items. The selection may be inconsistent, but you may find exactly what you are looking for. Some charities take in items from construction sites where a home is being renovated or torn down and they sell them at very inexpensive prices as their cost basis is zero. Believe it or not, some very costly items are available at these organizations if they are near affluent areas. You would be amazed at what people throw away! Some items are simply mistakes which were rejected and discarded even though they are new items!

As the saying goes, some people have more time than money and these suggestions will come in handy for those wanting to start their improvements sooner rather than later, depending on their financial situation.

When it comes to labor charges, you will find that it's much easier to ask a carpenter to adjust an existing door in your house which sticks a little, while he is already there installing three other doors. He may not even charge you, depending on the complexity of what needs to be done. Sometimes you just need to tighten some stripped hinge screws by plugging the screw holes with some shaved splinters of wood (some use golf tees!) and reinstalling the screws so they are tight to the jamb and hold the door firmly in place. This can take 5 minutes and sometimes there is no charge--because the carpenter is already there and wants to spread a little goodwill. If, however, you just needed that done and nothing else, you'll have to pay for the time to do that work. It's difficult for subcontractors to make a living doing 5 minute jobs here and there and setting up their equipment over and over again in the same day. That's why there can be a huge difference in price for very small jobs depending on if the subcontractor is already on the job and set up and ready to go. Don't assume that anything is free just because it is a small job, by the way, let the subcontractor make that call and accept any favors with gratitude. By being polite and appreciative, you'll be amazed at how may extras come your way without any additional charges. If you only knew how many people were invoiced each day for minor adjustments here and there--just because they were rude--you would be amazed...

I was managing a job once where the homeowner had been the president of a company who was currently negotiating a new job with another company and consequently, had some free time while he was sorting it all out. So, he was on the jobsite quite a bit. The project was going very smoothly and he really liked our subcontractors and he decided to barbecue some stunningly delicious gourmet hamburgers on a Friday for all of the guys working on the job that day. To say these were incredibly fantastic burgers was an understatement. They caught us all off guard with how good they were. This sincere gesture of kindness made quite an impact on the subcontractors and you can bet he didn't get charged for a whole series of extras after that day.

Was this manipulative or just smart? I'll let you decide, but for the price of some lean sirloin and some great condiments, the guys really had a sincere appreciation for this client and enjoyed working on his house more than any other project at the time. It was no coincidence that wherever this guy worked over the last decade, he was usually the President of the company. I'd say this was, at the very least, an example of how to motivate people.

4 I have a project in mind. Where do I start?

The best advice I can give anyone on this broad question is to start with an architect. You may think an architect is only for people who are building a new house, but that's not the case. If you're modifying your house to any appreciable degree, such as making it larger or moving some interior walls which are load bearing, your local building and zoning department will require a drawing so they can study your exact intentions. That's where an architect will come into the picture. Architects are your best chance at creative solutions to whatever improvements your home needs at the moment. A good architect is a priceless part of any successful project. Find a good one and your project will immediately have an enormous advantage no matter how small it is. In some cases, you will have no choice but to hire an architect to draw up your project so that it can be submitted to your local building and zoning department for a building permit. In other cases, like renovating your kitchen or master bathroom, you will be well served with an architect's expertise there too. Their ability to analyze spaces, proportions, lighting, practicality and minimum clearances is essential and if you are not trained in these areas, you could easily make a costly error on your own. Even if you just want some built-in shelves to flank your fireplace, do yourself a favor and seek out an architect's advice. You will be glad you did.

How do you find one? If you plan on being your own GC, then you can find an architect just like any other competent subcontractor, by checking some logical sources for names. First of all, ask your friends or co-workers, as long as you can inspect the work personally that was done. If you get the old "My nephew is a great architect, here's his number" routine and they have never actually hired their nephew to do anything, this is a paper thin endorsement of his credentials. You want names of architects who designed elements of people's homes or their entire home which you can inspect personally before you call that architect, or in some cases, after you call that architect, depending on the circumstances.

What if you don't have these kind of connections, or the work you see is subpar work? Visit your local building and zoning department and ask them in person for some advice on who does great work on residential projects. They see the drawings and inspect the projects of many different architects each day and they can give you some names. Be polite and diplomatic how you approach this question as some department personnel are sensitive to appear to be favorable toward any particular architect. If they have to give you several names to not appear to be partial, take them all. I always like to ask people in a position to give me advice, "If it was your house, who would you choose?"

Local building and zoning departments are a very useful place for you to get familiar with. Their personnel are generally very friendly and able to help you in countless ways. It would be appropriate to run anything you intended to do to your home by them first, so that they can advise you even before you submit an application for a building permit. They often respect you more for walking in to ask their advice because so many homeowners despise having to ask anyone's permission to do something to their own house and then pay a fee for it, so they try to do things secretly. Building departments are not happy when that happens. Some have had to lay off personnel in recent years because the soft economy has reduced building permit applications and in turn the fees that these generate. As local municipalities trim their budgets, people have lost their jobs. So when homeowners try to modify their homes without permits, reducing the revenue for their departments further, this grates on their nerves.

For the record, anyone who has work done to their home without a permit is taking a very unnecessary risk. Permits involve inspections by the local building and zoning department and inspections are for your safety. Sometimes talented subcontractors make unintentional mistakes and you need this safety net to catch these before they are dangerous. Unless you are an electrician, you may not spot a potential problem in a wiring job being done to your home and if the problem is not corrected, it could result in getting shocked or creating a fire inside a wall while you slept. Does it make sense how important it is to have another set of eyes looking for anything out of whack before the walls are closed up again and it's too late? Inspections prevent mishaps. Permits involve inspections. Permits are an important part of any construction.

So, when you walk in as a homeowner who wants to be above board and get a building permit and do things the right way, they respect that. You're one of the reasons they'll keep their job. You will find them to be very helpful as you navigate the process of doing your project. They can help you understand your zoning requirements, help you fill the application out, look up the file for your property and much more.

Many times, the project you have in mind will require an architect to study the plat of survey for your property--especially if you plan on adding on to it. This is the bird's eye view of your property showing its boundaries on each side and where your home is situated. There are lots of other useful details on this document as well, like the location of gas lines, underground power lines, sewer pipes and water pipes. All of these utility issues need to be taken into consideration if you intend to expand the footprint of your house and its foundation.

For example, you will have to re-route some of these pipes and wires ahead of time to accommodate the new excavation needed for the new foundation if these wires and pipes currently cross over where you want to build out. The plat shows a general idea of where the underground utilities are, but this should always be confirmed before any digging. There are utility locator services which will use electronic locator equipment to precisely mark where underground utility lines exist by ground level flags and spray paint. The color of the flags and spray paint used corresponds to the specific utility being located. Your excavator knows this is necessary for a safe dig and now you do too. Communicate with the excavator as to the need to mark the utilities in the exact area where the dig will occur.

In most areas, the excavator has to call this request into the location service, for insurance and procedural purposes. Make sure he specifically requests the back of the house to be marked if the digging will take place in the back of the house. I have seen instances where the utilities are clearly marked from the street to the front of the house and not marked in the back of the house, which can lead to some unfortunate digging accidents if buried power lines or gas lines are cut by a backhoe bucket. Even cable TV and internet wires have become vital to the way our homes are connected to the outside world and careful measures are needed to not sever these important lines of communication when they are buried.

The plat of survey is important for a number of reasons. The best place to look for your plat of survey is in the large folder you received when you bought the property, but if you can't locate it, the building department might have a copy in your property's file. Not always, mind you, but many times they have a copy of the plat of survey and can copy one for you. Any time the dimensions of the house are expanded on the lot, a new survey is required, so there may be several versions of the survey in your file if the house was added on to over the years several times. Look for the most current version and compare it to your house configuration to make sure. When all else fails, you can have a survey company come out and measure your property and create a new plat of survey. Before you go to this extent, make sure the project you intend to do is even feasible (albeit with an approved permit) by the building and zoning department. Talk it over with them first.

They may also have a copy of your original architectural drawings for your house. Again, not always, but many times they will. Or, at least they will have a copy of the drawings where an addition was added in more recent years since it was built, if it was an older home.

This will be a valuable document to have to start any project. The architectural plans to your house are a fantastic starting point to look over and study for ways to make any changes. Obtaining these if you don't already have them is a huge advantage, so look into your home's file at your local building and zoning department and get yourself a copy. If you can't locate them, it's not the end of the world. The architect can simply measure and draw up your floor plan as it exists today and start to look at your options from there.

When you get those names for the architects, invite them over for a visit and clarify if this is a paid consultation or not. You will want to do this in order to avoid any misunderstandings, especially if you are working on a modest budget. Discuss your needs with them and ask them to verbalize what they would recommend. Let them sketch something crudely during you visit if they choose to, but if not, don't insist on it. Architects are wary of homeowners who bleed them for advice, or insist on a brief sketch without a contract and then get their less talented "nephew" to draw up their ideas for less money. Be aware of that as you visit with them and be respectful of the ways they are guarded at times without any financial commitment from you.

Hire the one you can speak to the most comfortably and who has the best ability to communicate their ideas, even if they are slightly more expensive than the rest. This is not the contractor to "skimp" on. Which heart surgeon do you want--the cheapest or the best? Ask about how they would charge for the work and if they would stop by during the construction phase and if that was an additional charge. Ideally, you would want one set fee to cover doing the drawings and also stopping by during the construction if any work site questions arose--which always happens, by the way.

A reasonable payment schedule is 1/3 initial deposit. The next 1/3 comes due when the drawings are created to represent the basic layout of what you want. This is called the "Schematic Design" phase. The next phase is further refinement of the schematic design toward the "Conceptual Design" phase. Once the conceptual design phase is approved, the drawings are further refined to include more detailed information necessary to build from and for the permit submission process. This final phase is the "Construction Drawings" phase. The final 1/3 is typically due when these are complete and ready to submit to the building and zoning department. This final version of the drawings is detailed enough to submit for the permit application, pass out to the subcontractors for precise bids and to eventually build from.

A good architect can council you through the design process and communicate on your behalf to the building and zoning department to help you achieve your building permit. Many can let you know even before you get started drawing anything if your intended project can be accomplished or not, based on the building and zoning laws as they relate to your intentions. They can typically answer a myriad of questions for you during the design process and the construction process as well, so they are a very helpful resource to have access to when taking on a project. Good architects can even be a source to you for suggestions about competent subcontractors. They see a lot of work out there and they see who builds it and who is good at capturing the essence of the design and who is not.

The bottom line: Find a good architect and you will have a legitimate starting point for your project and be starting off with your best chance for achieving excellence. Don't be alarmed about never having studied construction drawings. The architect can explain every line, symbol and nuance and you will find them quite logical and intuitive very quickly.

5   How do I find the right subcontractors in terms of competence and price?

This is one of the most important reasons to Think like a General Contractor. Where do you find the best subcontractors? Let's consider your options. You could look in the phone book. You'll see dozens of choices. What now? Should you call the 23 plumbers in the plumbing section and start interviewing them? That would be a waste of time, believe me.

How about looking on the internet. Some websites offer special lists which promise the best subcontractors already pre-screened. Well, get out your wallet, because many of these sites charge you a fee for this. How do they select these subcontractors? Don't get me started... All I can say is follow the money...

Some websites are free to you, but charge the subcontractors to be listed on them. How do they select their subcontractors? Don't get me started... All I can say is follow the money...

The best subcontractors don't need to advertise. They treat people well, do solid work for a fair price and their reputations spread and perpetuate their business automatically as a result. They never have to go chase new business leads, the leads come to them. Those are the guys you want. How do you find them?

One way is to ask your friends who have used a plumber they liked. This is a good option, as they have seen their work and experienced how the plumber did business. Are your friends experts on plumbers? How do you know they didn't over pay? How do you know the work was done properly? Do you really trust your friend's expertise? Maybe yes, and that's great if you have a friend like that. Get that plumber's number and call them up and describe what you want to do. But first and foremost, ask them this critically important question up front: Do you have current liability and worker's compensation insurance? Can you please fax me a certificate? If they answer anything but "yes" move on. I don't care how good they are, if they are not properly insured, they are a huge liability risk for you and you should not accept that when managing your project. The good subcontractors are insured. Period. Even if the guy is your neighbor...get an insurance certificate.

As an aside, you will be very smart to actually have your own fax machine at home. They are incredibly cheap (some less than $100) and incredibly useful for this purpose. If you want important documents like insurance certificates and subcontractor bids to get to you quickly and easily, buy a fax machine. It's not smart not to have one and you will find other uses for it on a personal level which come in handy as well, so you will be glad you have one. These days, they are by no means an extravagance, but a necessity. You absolutely need one to be your own General Contractor.

If you get an insurance certificate for the sub on your fax machine in a day or so, invite them over for a site visit and explain in more detail what you want done and ask them to create a bid for you. If you go through the trouble of seeing them, getting a bid and wasting your time only to learn they can't produce an insurance certificate to prove they have it, you just delayed your project. When you don't know people, they need to start providing reasons for you to trust them and this is the first example of how they can earn your trust. The certificate should show both types of insurance, complete with start and end dates for the policy and a policy number for each one--liability and worker's compensation. If you get a certificate you can send it to your own insurance agent for advice about how to read it and check it for authenticity. See the pattern here: Consult experts on their field of expertise and you will always be well advised to proceed. This is an extremely useful skill to develop. Be sure to discuss your intentions to manage a project to improve your home with your insurance agent as well, to make sure you are carrying the proper insurance coverage to keep you protected.

Note: getting insurance certificates is a simple phone call for subcontractors to their insurance agent and they get this request all the time. The agent gets your fax number from the subcontractor and sends you the certificate. It's that simple. If the guy doesn't get you a certificate after assuring you he has insurance, it's a red flag. If he doesn't have insurance and can't prove it, move on. Chances are, your friend hired them and didn't even check. Most people don't even know to check, so this would not be uncommon. I don't care if he did a great job and was cheap. Move on. This is a risk you don't want to take.

The insurance issue alone is a filter separating good subcontractors from the bad ones. They might not have insurance because they are broke, which means they don't have enough work, which often means they are not very good, or just irresponsible. Others may not have it because they had too many claims and can't get an affordable policy now, or any policy. Wouldn't you want to know that before you trusted someone to work on your house? You risk an awful lot if this guy gets hurt accidently or intentionally, or makes a huge mistake and damages your house. His liability policy will help him pay for your damaged marble floor if he drops a pipe wrench on it while working on your master bathroom, or the damaged dining room floor if he causes a leak in a pipe which drips down on it. Do you know the plumber often uses a blowtorch to solder copper water pipe sections together? Do you really want a guy holding a blowtorch inside your bathroom walls without insurance? There are too many good subcontractors out there with insurance to take a risk on someone who doesn't. When you think like a GC, you don't take unnecessary risks.

If you decide to work with this guy and come to terms, ask, as a condition of the contract, to be "named as an additional insured" on his insurance policy. This means a small charge for him which won't break him, but it also puts you in line to receive notification if he ever cancels his policy without notice or gets dropped. You will be alerted immediately if you are an additional insured. You will get another certificate with this information clearly printed on it when you ask for this. It's the only way to confirm it was done. Some guys buy a policy to get a job, then cancel it the next day. Sound slimy? It is, so protect yourself. There is an inside game to every profession and part of this book is to expose some of the crooked moves that get pulled out there so you can always be one step ahead and prepared.

What if you don't have a friend who has done business with the kind of subcontractor you need? What if there was a "free" and reliable way to find great subcontractors judged by experts day in and day out who saw their work up close? Would you consider this? You should, it's called your local building and zoning department. Ask their inspectors for names of credible subcontractors. They inspect their work regularly and know the good ones from the bad ones. The people in your local building and zoning department will be tremendously valuable to you in this regard. Most will be more than willing to help you out and give you some names. Try to get multiple names for each subcontractor you need, for multiple bids. You can also ask your architect. Architects see a lot of different subcontractor's work and can be another good source of leads for good subcontractors for your project.

We're only a few chapters into the book and you already know some of the ways to save money and avoid service calls when possible. You have also learned exactly how to add to your knowledge about your home easily and effectively with experts, how to protect yourself from uninsured accidents and how to locate the best subcontractors. We're just getting started.

The first filter for a subcontractor is if he did good work for someone who knows what good work looks like. The second is if he has insurance. The third will be cost.

Cost is always important. You will at times find some subcontractors within pennies of each other in terms of cost. Sometimes, they will be thousands apart. The latter scenario will require you to understand why. When a wide disparity happens, there are some not so obvious reasons as to why.

The guy who comes in way cheaper may be doing so because he missed some important details of your intended scope of work. He may have left those out and as a result is much cheaper than his competitor. Be careful. You have to read every bid very carefully because only the details which makes it to that document will be executed if you sign it. So, if the trim carpenter agreed to install casing around 14 windows and you have 19 windows to trim, you will be out of luck if you sign his contract for 14. There will be no arguing, he agreed to 14 in the contract and you have 19, so too bad, you will have to pay him more for 5 more windows if he trims them. This is sometimes a deceptive technique and sometimes an honest mistake, so in either case, you need to read through the bids and carefully scrutinize if it represents what you need.

How do you do that? The drawings you have the architect prepare show the details which need to be built. You make sure every detail for every trade is accounted for. If your project involves 19 new windows, make sure that you know that number and that it shows up in writing when you read the trim carpenter bid. If your drawings show 24 new power outlets and 9 new light switches, makes sure the electrician has that understood and straight in his bid. If you are uncomfortable reading the construction drawings and want to make sure you understand the list of issues that those drawings are communicating correctly, simply have a meeting with the architect and ask them to help you make an exhaustive list of line items you need to get bids for to actually build the design. You are constantly comparing the scope of work in your drawings to the bids. If you do not have drawings, you should have a standard sheet which describes the scope of work that you pass out to each subcontractor so everyone is on the same page--literally. Think of this part as like that of a teacher grading term papers. Each student was given the parameters of the assignment and you have to determine if their paper fulfilled the criteria.

Some bids, like the trim material bid, should be cross checked by the trim carpenter. Trim suppliers are notorious for deleting some of the material you need and lowering their bid to win the contract. You get into the construction and you find out you're 145 feet short on crown molding. They know you'll just go ahead and order it and be too distracted by everything else to make a big deal out of it. That's slimy, but it happens. Measure your drawings to make sure your trim material (like base board molding, door and window casing and crown molding) is all accounted for to the exact linear foot. One way to confirm this is to have the trim carpenter do a "take off" (an assessment of the drawings for a bid) to measure out each issue and account for the proper amount of material to be ordered. The trim carpenter often does this anyway to assess his bid costs. Use his extra set of eyes to confirm your numbers for the trim material as a double check.

When you are convinced each bid is accurate and they are from competent subcontractors, then the lower cost bid becomes the value play. That is, if all of the terms are the same as the other bids. Specifically, if you aren't asked for a deposit from any other subcontractor, but the lowest bid asks for 20% down, then this becomes an issue to discuss. Ask him to waive the deposit if he wants your business, then he has the deal. Be ready to sign the contract with that change made (he marks it and initials it and you do too) if he agrees. Don't ask for a concession and then say you'll think about it, get down to business with the guy and close the issue. Treat these guys with respect and don't toy with them. You want to set a tone of being fair, smart and respectful. This alone will improve the quality of work you generate when you get the right guys signed up to do the job. A good deal is a good deal if it's good for both parties, not just one. If you think you're smart if you catch a guy off guard and he agrees to a job for a lot less than he should have, you're not. He will become unmotivated quickly and this will impact the quality of the work he does. Carefully lock in each contract making sure it's accurate, complete and a reasonable cost for you and the subcontractor.

The point is, be conscious of and protective of every subcontractor's morale as you choose them and bring them into your project. To the extent that it's reasonable, try to make them *want* to work on your project and you will be all the closer to achieving excellence.

If you mistakenly think the path to saving money is to be demeaning toward those you hire and driving bargains down their throats and asking for extra work at no charge and reminding them of the state of the economy and the privilege they have in working on your project, you will learn a hard lesson. They will fire *you*. Maybe it won't happen in an obvious way. Maybe they will just stop showing up consistently, or at all, right when you need them most. Believe me, they know exactly when to not show up to disrupt the momentum of your project.

The path to excellence is paved with due diligence on who you hire and lots of "please" and "thank you's" along the way long after you hire them. You don't have to patronize them, but look a guy in the eye when you speak to him and let him reply without interruption and always be respectful. You would be surprised at how many additional notches of effort you will gain from each subcontractor you choose as a result...without costing you another dime. I told you I would explain how to save money, this is how you do it. As the project goes along and you establish respect with each sub, they will often not charge extra for some extra work details which come up as the project proceeds. It's just a good policy for a number of reasons and I can't stress it enough.

Let's discuss more about achieving the best price for a moment. You will find, when you ask for multiple bids, that there can be a disparity. Make certain that you understand the underlying reason for the disparity. Every bid comes down to labor and material charges. Ask to see those separated and compare your bids. It's a tedious part of Thinking like a General Contractor, but maybe the most important part. Everything you do must somehow make its way to a contract in writing which the subcontractor will agree to for a certain dollar amount. Pour over the bids to see if they are first and foremost, complete and accurate. If they pass that litmus test, then compare them to competing bids and if there is a disparity, pick up the phone and discuss it with the individual subcontractors. Explain that you just want to make a good decision and want to understand each bid as clearly as possible. Ask why their bid is so much lower or higher than the competitor's bids after if you confirm it to be complete, then ask how they manage that. If you have a low bid, ask if you can expect the work to start and continue uninterrupted until completion. See if they would be willing to make that an addendum to the contract. Now would be a good time to ask how long the work would take under reasonable conditions. Listen to how the subcontractor handles them self during this call and use your gut to sort through the ones you feel are up to the task and the ones you should pass on. When everything else is equal, use your gut instinct to decide between which subcontractor to hire.

Don't be afraid to approach a higher priced subcontractor (who you would prefer to do the work because they are superior at it) and level with them about price. Make it clear that you respect their abilities, but you have bids for substantially less. Ask if they have any room to move on price, but be polite about it. Stress that you want the contract to be a good one and that means good for both parties, not just you. See what they say.

Nine times out of ten, if you approach this issue with proper respect and allow the subcontractor the chance to gracefully lower their price, they will. You'll see. Don't insist that they "meet" the competitor's price, simply state the competitor's price and ask if they could move on theirs. If they do, you have just successfully negotiated a superior subcontractor to lower their price, which is great news for you. If they move at all, this is a victory. If they agree to a price just above their competitor's price, this is ideal. You are paying a slight premium and acknowledging their superior skill in doing so and they have no reason to be offended by your approach as they are still doing the work for more money than their competitor.

People who cram "take it or leave it" offers down subcontractors throats are short sighted and will start the job off on the wrong foot. You don't want to create this kind of atmosphere on your job site. It will harm your results and leave you way short of achieving excellence. The subcontractors talk to each other on the job site and you need them in a positive frame of mind when they show up, so their quality of work and their cooperation are at their peak levels on your job.

As you zero in on each subcontractor, you should be loading this information into a master spreadsheet. If you are not familiar with how to use spreadsheet software programs, take the time to learn. They are extremely useful. You will absolutely need a spreadsheet program to Think like a General Contractor and there is no avoiding it. Each line item is a category of the construction project that needs to be accomplished by a specific subcontractor. Even modest projects will involve 8 or 10 subcontractors and suppliers. You need to be able to add these bids together with perfect and instant accuracy and keep their payments straight and orderly as well. You always want to know where you are financially at any moment and the spreadsheet can deliver this information to you each day instantly. Good spreadsheet software makes this effortless. You can even size up an estimated cost scenario to see if you even want to go through with your project in the first place. It's how you define a project and make sure you have all the elements covered and what the total costs are. Just because you have something drawn up by an architect, does not mean that you will be able to afford to do it and the spreadsheet helps clarify this and helps you calculate some ways to possibly break the project into phases to make it more affordable. Spreadsheet software is essential to a GC and you will be glad you took the time to learn it if you don't use it already in your career. It's the essence of business: What does the project cost? Where can we save? Where can we afford to spend more? Can we afford this today? Tomorrow? In a year? What are the most significant costs of the project? Can we leave anything out for now to be added later?

The spreadsheet is your financial framework for the project. It's your radar screen of costs and can help you make any number of better decisions. Show me a GC who does everything with yellow legal pads and a calculator and I'll show you a guy who makes costly mathematical mistakes, can't experiment with different cost options quickly and accurately and has a hard time keeping track of things in general. Even a modest project could involve hundreds of calculations and recalculations of cost. Rely on the spreadsheet software to make them for you instantly and accurately, which is the only way to operate a job site in an orderly fashion.

As you add information to the spreadsheet from the subcontractor bids you inclined to choose, you will start to see the financial shape of the project start to come into focus. The more line items you can fill in with legitimate bid numbers, the more accurate your actual project budget becomes. This is extremely important information as you may decide to trim back the project's scope of work because it's exceeding what you can afford. Or, you may be coming in under what you can afford and can add to the project if you choose to do so. The point is, you have to know where you are at all times when it comes to the budget, so you can make any adjustments necessary to accomplish your goals, or modify your goals.

There are no exceptions to this reality. If you want to manage a project effectively, you half to be able to make cost calculations instantly and accurately and you can't do that with a yellow legal pad and a calculator. Thinking like a GC means managing enormous amounts of information accurately to the penny at all times. The ongoing cost analysis of the project is every bit as important as the design and the quality of work. You will be totaling and re-totaling the bids constantly until you start the job and once you do, you will need to track exactly how much work is done by each subcontractor and what percentage of their contract they are entitled to be paid up to that moment. If the electrician accomplishes 25% of his work by the time you are ready to make your first progress payments at the first 30 day payment interval, you should pay him 25% of his contract.

At the risk of belaboring the point, I just want to stress that you can't "wing it" on this aspect of the GC role. This is not a casual part of the job, it's the essence of the job. It can be a tedious part too, which is why some GC's are undisciplined about it and take their focus off the daily need to update the spreadsheet and let a few days or weeks slip by because they don't feel like sitting at a computer each day. The result is often some unintended cost overruns which were decisions made on in the field verbally and never recorded in the spreadsheet and never formally agreed to in writing with the subcontractors. When this happens, you can be guaranteed the subcontractors will think they are owed more money than you do as you try to piece together verbal exchanges from 3 weeks ago when it comes time to pay them.

Don't let this happen. It's a nightmare and will cost you. I've seen GC's lose their bearings and the next thing you know the subcontractors are walking off the job and some will even file liens against the property until they are paid what they feel they are owed.

6   How should I pay the subcontractors?

You should pay every subcontractor every 30 days. This is a very reasonable interval. During those 30 day windows, if their contracts are changed in any way with extras or deletions, this should be reflected in writing in their specific contract file on your desk with a document from them stating the change you both agreed to. These are called "change orders." Any changes should then be carried over to the master spreadsheet. You always want an accurate depiction of every subcontractor's contract available to you at a glance on the master spreadsheet. For example, the painter's contract is $4,750, but we added 2 more rooms to that, for $875 more, so his contract is $5,625 in total and he has completed 20% of the job so far and is entitled to a 20% payment of $1,125, leaving $4,500 left on his contract. Simple math, that's all.

We discussed the need for spreadsheet proficiency, the need for a fax machine and now we'll need to make sure you have an email address. I assume that you do, as most of the population has come this far, at least, in technological advancement. That's a plus if you do, because you will need it. You will need to communicate with the subcontractors before during and after the project and this is a very efficient way to do that. Some still prefer the fax machine, but many will be sending you their bids and change orders at times, via email. They sometimes send their bids as email attachments. Make sure you understand how to open these and read them and be able to send attachments of your own too. Everything you do should have written documentation.

Show me a project which went way over budget and I'll show you a GC who was probably at the bar having a cold one each afternoon when he should have been at his desk sorting through the changes and updates of the day's activity. This is more often the case than you realize, which is why it is so beneficial for you to understand the responsibilities of the GC job. The "second half" of my day often starts after 6pm when I make it back to my desk from being on the jobsite and make my list of subcontractors who owe me change orders, download digital pictures of areas in question regarding quality on the job site which get emailed to specific subcontractors and the architect, update the spreadsheet, study the change orders I just received for accuracy, communicate any errors on the change orders, communicate progress updates to the subcontractors who need to start their phase next, answer any questions raised on the job site which required more research and so on. I keep a record of problems to solve each day and update that record constantly. I also make appointments to see certain subcontractors or suppliers at the job site at certain times and keep those records on my smart phone. I also save emails in specific files for each job so I can reference them in the event of any future "misunderstandings."

You need technology to help you keep all of this straight. Technology is your ally in this undertaking and you should make sure you are at least up to speed on the basic tools and software which are widely used today. Many of you already are and are therefore all the more prepared to take this on.

Once you agree to a contract, most labor intensive subcontractors like framing carpenters should not require a down payment or a deposit and they should be comfortable with starting the job and receiving their first check at the regular 30 day window. You can even make a case that a plumber does not necessarily need a down payment even though they have to buy some rather costly material up front to start the job. If you are committed to a 30 day window in terms of payment, this is a reasonable amount of time for them to buy the material on credit and pay their material bill after receiving their payment from you. This is another reason for you to have a legitimate 30 day payout interval. Sometimes, if the payout interval is 45 days, you will have a difficult time eliminating deposit requirements. If you can avoid them, you should.

Now, on this subject, the best subcontractors pay their suppliers and have good credit relationships with them. However, some suppliers have recently changed their credit rules and require all subcontractors to sign unreasonable credit agreements which hold them personally liable for the payment of the supplies even if they are not paid by the client, in this case, you--the GC. There have been so many defaults in recent years due to the economy and some flat out dishonesty, the suppliers are having to ratchet up their rules. Some subcontractors refuse to take this risk for a client anymore. After not being certain that they will be paid for a job that they just spent money on, they will insist on a deposit. Don't fight this, but make sure it's reasonable and explained and correlates to the bid. If there is $985 worth of materials involved and they ask for a $4,000 deposit, that's a red flag. Accept a $985 deposit requirement as being reasonable if all of the material will be purchased in the first 30 days. Insist on getting an original, signed, notarized "material lien waiver" when you pay them the deposit which is intended for materials to be purchased. We'll cover more on waivers in a moment.

You want to prevent releasing a dime to any subcontractor unless they have done some work, with the only exception being substantial material purchases they need to make. Make their payment terms part of your initial discussions with them and take the time to clarify them. Many will spell their terms out on their bid document. Know that at times, they spell out aggressive terms as a cookie cutter paragraph on their bid, like " 20% down, another 30% at the first payout , 40% at the second payout and 10% final. This is all well and good, but you want to insist that you will pay for reasonable material costs up front, provided they are justified and accounted for (accompanied by material lien waivers) and will pay anything else based on progress alone. If they only accomplish 5% of the work by the time the first payout takes place, that is a reasonable percentage of their contract to pay and nothing more, with zero exceptions.

Don't try to be too clever on this detail. If you pay less than what they are owed, this is not fair and somewhat insulting and they might roam off to jobs where they can get paid more fairly and your project will suffer. If you pay more than they are owed up to that point, they also don't have much incentive to return and finish promptly and might chase down new projects while they have a cushion of money in their pocket. You want them to return and be paid exactly the percentage of work they have accomplished up to that point so they always have the incentive to finish. Explain to everyone that is how you do business and be clear, but respectful about it and they will acquiesce 99.9% of the time to your terms. Anyone who does not agree with this should likely not be working for you. The paragraphs in their bids are merely an attempt to tilt the terms in their favor so they are paid slightly in advance of doing the work, which is never a good idea. Cross out those terms and write "progress percentage payments" when you sign their contract. This means they will be paid the same percentage as their progress. Make sure they agree to that and initial that.

Let's talk about some important issues to cover when you actually pay the subcontractors a reasonable percentage of their contract. For the purpose of making the point, let's talk about what not to do first. Let's say you want some simple wooden shelves installed in your garage for storage and you hire some local handyman who worked on your neighbor's house last summer fixing his mailbox. This guy is a nice old man with a trustworthy face and overalls and a pickup truck loaded with tools.

What if everything goes smooth and your handyman builds these shelves and you pay this handyman $200 and a month later, you find out he filed a lien on your property for $200 and claims you never paid him and he refuses to release the lien until you do pay him--even though you have a canceled check! How can you protect yourself?

Do you know what a notarized final lien waiver is? If you don't, you are taking a risk by paying any contractor who works on your house. They can file a lien for very little money and they don't even need an attorney in many states. They know it will cost you more in legal fees to fight them in court and that it would be cheaper to just pay them $200 in exchange for their lien release. They can claim you had a verbal agreement and you can pay your attorney a few grand to defend you in court and roll the dice that the judge might actually think this charming little old handyman was actually jilted out of $200 by *you* and order *you* to pay up.

Pretty slimy, huh. Even if you win the case, you have your time and legal fees gone forever. A good GC makes sure any subcontractor who receives a single dime in payment provides the properly signed and notarized partial or final lien waivers at the exact moment they are paid. This is a legal document signed by the subcontractor and witnessed by a notary public for being authentic . It declares that they have been paid. Even honest subcontractors make mistakes and forget to mark your bill as "paid" in their records even though they were paid. Then, when they close their books for the year, they confront you with your "outstanding invoice." Showing them their signed, notarized waiver settles this matter instantly.

A waiver is a signed, notarized legal document which states in a very formal and indisputable way that the subcontractor has been paid what they are owed and is therefore "waiving" (willingly giving up) their rights to file a lien against your property.

A lien is a powerful tool whereby the subcontractor communicates in writing with the county record department that they are still owed the amount shown on the lien for work performed. This lien becomes part of your property's title records. The lien signifies part "ownership" which they now have in your property up to the amount which they are owed. This will become an issue if you ever want to refinance or sell your property as this lien will show up on your title search report and have to be paid off or released by a notarized lien release by the subcontractor before the bank will allow your refinance or sale to go through. Anytime you go through a refinance or a sale, your title records are searched by the lender for unresolved issues just like this. In some states, liens are so powerful, the subcontractor can file one and then start foreclosure proceedings to sell your house out from under you to generate proceeds to pay off the lien. This is a complex process mind you and rarely ever happens and requires an expensive battle in court with extensive attorney fees which most subcontractors cannot afford. The idea is to avoid this altogether and insist on signed notarized lien waivers in exchange for payment for all subcontractors. This is just smart, regardless of how much money you have and are spending on subcontractors for work done.

Things happen, so protect yourself. Note: Only the original signed notarized waiver counts. So, they cannot fax this to you or email it to you or hand you a copy and keep their original. Only the original means anything in court. Get the original and read it before you hand some guy any money. Every dime you pay out to any subcontractor must be accounted for by a signed, notarized lien waiver. There are no exceptions to this, no amount too small, no situations where this can be safely avoided, if you want to protect yourself. A good GC always protects the title of the property which he is working on. This is the only way to do that.

Know that if you give an electrician $750 as a deposit for "materials" he needs to buy ahead of time, you must receive a signed, notarized material lien waiver. This is simply a lien waiver which describes who provided the material and that they were properly paid in full. If the electrician bought the material from a material supply company for your job, that material supply company should sign and notarize the material lien waiver. If the electrician simply gathered the supplies out of his own personal inventory of material, then the material lien waiver would come from him, signed by him and notarized. In either case, you need a material lien waiver if you advance anyone a dime to buy material. If not, the electrician could pick up the material on credit, install it in your house, take a deposit from you, not pay for the material, pocket the money instead and the material supply company could file a lien on your house until they are paid in full.

If you need further information on how to understand how waivers work, call a local title company and they can walk you through it. Partial lien waivers are required when you make a progress percentage payment and in that partial lien waiver is an agreed upon contract amount, how much you have paid, how much you are paying today and how much is owed. There is zero room for misunderstanding about payment issues. The lien waiver document is prepared, signed and notarized by the subcontractor and presented to you in person in exchange for the check from you. You need a final lien waiver if the payment you are making is your last payment to complete the contract or the there is only one payment when the contract is completed.

If you want to see what a legitimate signed, notarized lien waiver looks like, visit a title company close by and ask them to show you some examples. Title companies offer a wonderful service which comes in handy for when you get a more substantial project going someday down the road. When it comes time to pay your subcontractors, you pay the title company and the title company pays the subcontractors *only after* they provide properly prepared waivers. Title companies have blank waiver forms handy and notary publics to notarize them. This service will cost you a fee, but for ease of paying subcontractors safely it is absolutely the right thing to do. They worry through all those details for you, provided you update them with the state of every sub contractor's contract. I recommend to all of my clients to pay their bills for their project in this way. Some go through a title company, some just have me collect the waivers instead and they make the checks out every 30 days to the individual subcontractors. If you don't have the money to pay a title company fee for your project, you can easily insist on this procedure yourself and collect the waivers yourself to protect your home from fraudulent liens being filed by dishonest subcontractors. In so doing, you are protecting yourself like a title company would, but avoiding their fee. Good honest subcontractors still need to provide lien waivers. It's the only protective document that holds up in court proving that payment was made in case of a misunderstanding.

Don't be bashful about asking a guy for a waiver in exchange for even a small $50 payment you owe him. Some subcontractors will imply that it's not enough money to warrant a waiver because they don't like paperwork. That's just because they don't want to hassle with getting one written up and notarized. It's not a big deal for him to swing by any bank and have the bank's notary public witness his signature on his waiver and notarize it and then give it to you. If a subcontractor seems to not understand the lien waiver process, chances are they are not sophisticated enough to do business with. Direct them to a title company to get schooled up, or, explain it to them, or help them fill it out, or don't work with them. I've been through all of those scenarios, believe me. Also, some subs are a bit lazy about having blank waiver forms handy. I keep a blank form for a final waiver (this is used only when they are done with the job) and partial waiver (this is used to verify an incremental payment received during a job in progress) in a file on my computer and I email them to any sub who I am about to pay so they don't have any excuses about not having waivers. Even good subcontractors are at times ill prepared on this detail, which is ironic because they don't get paid until they take care of this. I also have some blank waiver forms in my truck. It's an important detail, but one that can sometimes get lost in the shuffle when the project gets rolling and people want to be paid. You can't let this slide. You have to protect your home's title from liens and this is your only protection, so embrace this and be safe. That's thinking like a GC.

I have had more conversations than I can count with people who were extremely wealthy and smart, but they couldn't resist hiring a guy "on the side" to do a job very cheaply. For example, they brag to me about how they hired one of their electrician's technicians to do install some exterior lights on the back of their house "on the side." This means they were not hired through the electrical company they are employed by, where they are fully protected and insured.

The technician does the work on a Sunday afternoon for example and gets paid a substantially reduced fee, in cash. Doing this through the electrical company where the tech works would be more expensive, but hiring the worker secretly is much less expensive, which is extremely attractive to naive homeowners. They often brag about their amazing abilities to save money to me in this way as if I should adopt this approach be as clever as they are. I just have to silently ponder the foolishness of this risk. You try to explain this to homeowners sometimes and very few of them get it, so you just give up and smile instead.

More importantly, can *you* see the risk here? The tech does not carry liability or worker's comp insurance for this kind of "under the radar" work and may be uncomfortable with any written record of the transaction such as a lien waiver. They will be working with electricity and on a ladder and often times without a necessary permit. Can you see all of the potential hazards here? And yet, as you read this sentence, some guy has both hands in an electric panel in a dark basement somewhere making some extra money "on the side" hoping nothing goes wrong...

The very same people who wouldn't dare take their Mercedes out of the garage if it was not fully insured, will have an uninsured guy clipping electric wires on a ladder in their backyard. Does this make sense? That's why it's time for homeowners to start to Think like a General Contractor. Some homeowners, frankly, need to be saved from themselves.

7 What is the typical chronology of the construction process?

After the drawings are submitted to the local building and zoning department, after the project has been communicated to each subcontractor and the winning bids have been scrutinized and selected, after the spreadsheet has been updated with all pertinent information to actually build the project, after the building and zoning department approves the project and the building permit, after the building permit is paid for and picked up, it's time to start. What happens now?

There are a few different starting points, depending on the nature of your project. First of all, pick a place for a nice portable toilet on or near your driveway for the subcontractors to use and have it delivered. Pick another spot for a dumpster to be parked during most of the project and make sure it's accessible for a large truck to pick up and deliver fresh, empty dumpsters as required. If you are adding on to your home and need to excavate, call the excavator and ask when they can start and have them call the utility locator service to mark the underground utility line locations in the spot they need to dig. Have the excavator meet you on the site to measure off the digging area and mark it with spray paint using your architectural drawings as your guide. If there are utility lines to move, call the corresponding utility services and ask them to help you coordinate this. If you are moving a power line, bring your electrician into this discussion. If you are moving a gas line, bring your plumber into this discussion. If you are moving a TV cable line, bring your cable service provider and your electrician into this discussion.

To save time, you would usually have the buried utility lines located weeks before you get your permit *after* you have discussed your project with the local building and zoning department and are confident they will approve it. You should start all of these discussions ahead of time with the utility companies so you understood the charges involved for doing this work and start their process to get it done as well. Working with utility companies takes a few weeks as they have to come out and look the site over, so the earlier you get started, the better. The utility companies are happy to help you move lines and happy to send you a bill for it. Get them working on this as soon as possible, it may take a month for them to actually do this work, from the time you initiate your first call, so these issues are ready to go when you pick up your permit.

When expanding your house's footprint, everything starts with the work do be done associated with the foundation. Identify if there are an obstructions which would get in the way of the excavation. These are typically underground utility lines, but may include having to move some landscaping features. You might have to remove shrubs and trees of a certain minimum diameter in trunk size will need permission from your local building and zoning department to remove or move or possibly replace. For example, you may have to remove a tree of 8 inches in diameter and the local building and zoning department may require you to plant 2 more new trees of a minimum of 4 inches in diameter each to replace them, somewhere else on your property. This will all be discussed in the process of them approving your building permit.

Depending on the complexity of your project and how busy the building and zoning department is at the time you submit your permit application, it may take a few days or a few weeks to actually get your permit. This sometimes involves having to make a slight change or two to your design in order to be compliant with current codes. Often (and this is a good thing) you will have to upgrade your smoke detector system if you work on your house. Local building and zoning departments sometimes have stricter guidelines on the level of sophistication your smoke detection system needs to be and they use the chance they have while you are renovating as the perfect time to have a new system installed as a mandatory requirement for your permit to be approved. Some will require a system that is hardwired with battery back-ups and connected to a phone line to dial the monitoring service so they can send police or fire department assistance. This is an extra expense, to be sure, but it prompts people to make their home safer. We regularly see systems that are inadequate by today's standards. As an aside, think about your own smoke detector system and make sure you have a smoke detector on every level and near every bedroom and there are fresh batteries in every unit. It's possibly the cheapest, most important thing you can do to protect your loved ones and it so often gets overlooked. Serviceable smoke detectors start at $5, so there is not a good excuse *not* to have them all over your home.

Once you get the permit and have your utility lines identified or trees identified or bushes or whatever may be in the way of the excavation, coordinate with the excavator to do some partial excavation to expose those lines so the utility companies can re-route them. Try to be there for that process as it is delicate and if the excavator sends only one person, it's always better to have someone else there to watch the bucket dig into the soil as they get closer to the utilities. The last bit of soil removed near utility lines needs to be done by hand with a shovel, so someone watching the process can help the back hoe operator spot what is going on and wave them off if they get near a line. Do you want things to go right and smoothly? The only way to make that happen is to physically be there during critical moments. This is one of them.

Once everything is moved or relocated where it needs to be to finish the dig, the excavator can finish creating the hole to the dimensions necessary to allow the concrete work. Note that the hole is always a couple feet larger than the dimensions of the concrete foundation, so there is room to work on setting up the foundation wall forms and also room to lay some new drain tile around the outermost perimeter of the new foundation to connect to the existing drain tile which surrounds the existing house. Drain tile protects the water below the surface from seeping into the basement under the walls. In theory, it catches the water before it seeps into the basement and re-routes it to a pit inside where it drains and accumulates and eventually gets pumped out. This is an extremely important feature for homes or additions with basements, as we discussed earlier, so your new basement will need this protection as well. Some foundations are merely some short walls surrounding unexcavated soil which stays put, with a shallow (3-4 inch) concrete floor poured over gravel which is spread on the unexcavated soil. This is a "slab" foundation and does not typically have a drain tile surrounding it because there are typically no water seepage issues in this kind of foundation. The only thing you need to worry about is making sure the soil around the home is at least 6 inches below the top of the foundation, so water does not collect and seep into the home as a result.

Consider this: Concrete foundations are generally created by three separate, consecutive pours:

1. The footings get poured first. Think of them as mini "sidewalks" about 12 inches thick and about 24 inches wide.

2. The concrete for the walls is poured next, inside the sturdy metal/wood forms which rest on top of the already hardened footings which were poured a day or two before.

3. Lastly, the floor or "slab" is poured once the walls are hardened enough to remove the forms. Sometimes, the slab is not poured and the dirt floor is left there instead, for a crawl space. This saves money, but causes a mess whenever work needs to be done under there. By pouring just a shallow (about 2 inches deep) floor also called a "slush coat" you can enable that crawl space to be used for storage and make it a lot easier to work under there for installing plumbing pipes

and electrical conduit. We don't recommend having a crawl space be just a dirt floor.

When you pour concrete in freezing temperatures, the ground can swell up and "heave" or move enough to disturb or crack the newly hardening concrete footings. The goal is to have the footings remain intact, as one solid, monolithic chunk of concrete. This will help the walls to stay firmly in place and not continue to sink or settle deeper into the soil. The longer the freezing temperatures have been lingering when the footings are poured, the more risk there is of heaving.

Sometimes, when footings are poured in the winter, the GC will have the last few inches of excavation done just a few hours before the concrete truck shows up so the soil is not exposed to the freezing temperatures long enough to start to freeze and "heave." This way, the forms for the footings can be built and ready for the concrete pour before the ground beneath them freezes. This involves a lot of weather report monitoring and coordination with the excavator and the concrete crew and the city inspector. The inspector needs to make that footing inspection as quickly as possible in freezing temperatures so the freshly poured footings can be covered to keep them warm. Sometimes, this is literally with blankets or a layer of straw. Either way, you want to protect the footings long enough to get the forms built for the walls, get the walls poured, the drain tile connected and inspected. The wall forms are removed from the hardening walls the next day, damp proofing sprayed on the new wall exteriors, optional foam board insulation attached to the exterior, drain tile covered with gravel and then backfilled with clay, then topsoil.

After this is complete, gravel is spread out over the dirt floor followed by a couple inches of fresh concrete to complete the concrete work. Once this is hardened up by the next day, you can walk on it to work in the basement. There might be windows to install and that can begin, or if the addition is large enough to warrant a steel beam to support the floor joists at the midway point of a span, this would be installed now as well. The beam would rest on the foundation walls in "pockets" which are predetermined notches in the foundation wall specifically to hold the beams. Sometimes the beam is supported by a steel column at its midway point for further support. Any steel work needed follows the concrete work.

Once the concrete foundation walls are up and you are backfilled and the steel (if any) is in place, you can have the framing carpenters start building the deck. They will bolt down a pressure treated (rot resistant) 2x4 or 2x6 on the perimeter of the foundation wall and nail in some rim (perimeter) joists and start nailing in the rest of the joists as well, followed by a plywood deck. Next, the walls go up and the roof structure follows. When this is all complete and the addition has the plywood on the walls and the roof and you have the windows installed and the roof material (for example, asphalt shingles) installed, you are "enclosed." You are ready for your framing inspection and once that is passed, you can have the plumber start his work, followed by the HVAC work, followed by the electrician--in that order. They have to go in that sequence because the plumber (if they need to be part of this addition) needs to have flexibility to run his pipes first as they are the most expensive and least flexible pipes. All this time, you can have the exterior siding installed and consider when you will "open" the house into the new addition. Next, the HVAC technician needs to run his vents, followed by the electrician who routes his conduit around their work. After everything is in place, you can have it all inspected and you are ready to close the walls with drywall. You can start cutting the existing house's exterior wall to connect into the new addition at this point or near this point. That will involve careful measures when cutting through existing water, sewer and power lines in that process. The insulation crew comes by at this point and gets the walls and ceiling insulated properly.

Once this is done, the existing house opening to the addition can be cleaned up and dry walled properly according to the plan. Once the new drywall's seams are mudded, taped and sanded, they can be primed and then it's time to get the flooring in place. Once the hardwood, tile, or laminate is installed, the trim carpenters can install the base molding, window casing, crown molding and any interior doors and their casing as well. If there is any cabinetry to install or custom built in shelves, it takes place at this point. While this is being done, the electricians can pull wire through the conduit they installed behind the drywall and they can install switches, receptacles and light mounting boxes. After that, the painters paint the room and the electricians come back to get the light fixtures installed.

At this point all that should be needed is the furniture!

On the other hand, if your project does not involve any concrete work, you would start by laying down some protection on the floors where the path from the project to the dumpster outside would be. We sometimes tape down two layers of paper, then thin plywood over that, depending on the situation. You want to map out the best path from the work area to the dumpster and know ahead of time that this path will be traveled by many subcontractors in boots, in all sorts of weather, so you need the floor covered with something that can stand up to that. If there is carpet involved in this path, it should be covered in the sticky (on one side) plastic wrap. If the carpet will be ripped out as part of the renovation, obviously it does not need to be covered at all. If you intend to sand and refinish the hardwood floor, cover it anyway. You don't want dropped tools dinging it up. Play it safe. Cover tile with paper and plywood. Keep it safe from a dropped tool. Even careful subcontractors drop a tool now and then and you have to keep the floor protected.

Once you have everything covered, you can begin "demolition." This is where any cabinets coming out are removed, walls taken apart, old windows, sections of ceiling and walls taken out to accommodate "behind the wall" work like plumbing, HVAC and electrical. Anything that comes out and gets thrown away to make room for the new items, is the demolition stage and it is the beginning of most projects that do not involve concrete.

Obviously, once the new walls are up (if any) and work behind the walls is done, the work is inspected and you start to close things up and proceed as described earlier. Protect, remove, open up, close up, move on...

8   How do I estimate the time to do the whole job?

You can tap several sources for estimating the time for the project. First of all, you can ask the city building and zoning department what they think a job like yours should take based on what they have seen for similar projects. Second, you can ask the framing carpenters what their experience says about the time needed for a job like yours. Third, you can ask how long each sub needs for each phase of the work and calculate it as a grand total for all of their collective efforts. In reality, the work often settles in at some sort of an average of all of those sources.

Issues which are hard to predict can slow the project down unexpectedly. It could snow 12 inches one night and you aren't able to get a delivery of lumber as a result of the road conditions, so you can't build anything because you're waiting on that lumber. You find out the tile you picked out was "said" to be in stock and it never was in stock and will take 7 weeks to arrive from Italy, so you can't install the tile. When you can't tile, you can't install cabinetry because they are consecutive issues, so there is a delay there and you can't finish the base molding or wainscoting because it runs into the cabinetry and terminates, so there is a domino effect as you are now faced with choosing a different, readily available tile in order to maintain progress.

Your windows may take 2-6 weeks to arrive, making it important to order them as soon as possible once you confirm that you are going through with the project and have the permit. If they are delayed, you can't do much past a certain point in the framing process, because you need the home to be water tight and fully enclosed in order to do those things. No sense in installing drywall if the rain will blow in and soak it and damage it. You may assume you can cover the window openings in the wall with plastic, but you would have to affix it to your new exterior siding with some penetrations (bad idea) and the bottom line is you need a legitimate window in that wall opening to keep the elements out, not a sheet of plastic. The goal is to achieve excellence and this is the path to excellence, not a path of "winging it," throwing up some plastic and hoping for the best...

The day you pick up the building permit, call in the order for the windows. By the time you are excavated, framed and ready, they should be on the jobsite ready to be installed. This is important, in order to not cause any delays in being "enclosed" so you can keep going.

Anything that you have to make a decision on is best to be decided upon before you even *start* the construction. This is how you avoid work stoppages. Ideally, you have all your cabinetry picked out and ordered, counter top material, flooring material, casing, base and crown profiles, plumbing and lighting fixtures too. The more you have picked out, the better, as you can start ordering these items to be delivered to the jobsite and stored in the garage, the house or a temporary storage container on the site. Any items requiring "lead time" should be closely monitored by you so that you are not slowing down the progress by waiting on an item. The sooner you order, the better. One possible exception is the appliances. They are installed last and it makes no sense having them delivered to the jobsite only to have to worry through keeping plastic on them and protecting them from the debris of the construction process. Coordinate with your appliance supplier to hand on to them until you need them. Expect them to be a little crabby about this as they want to deliver the items and collect the rest of their money after your deposit. They'll get over it. Don't bring your $10,000 oven to the jobsite and risk having it scratched by somebody's tool belt trying to squeeze by it in your crowded garage. Keep it at the appliance store until it's time to install it.

If you need to, use your spreadsheet listing all of the subcontractors for the job and rearrange them in chronological order of their work and the time they estimated they needed to complete their work and you will generate a total number of days on the bottom line for your job. Always add a month to this total and it will help give you a realistic completion date even with a few curve balls to deal with. Any delays in one part of the job even if its early on, delay the whole job. Don't expect the guys who do the last part of the job, like painting, to miraculously speed up their work so you can finish your project on time. It doesn't work that way and if you rush the guys at the end, you will get sloppy, hurried work at a critical phase of the project: The phase you see. The trim carpenters and painters need to take their time at the end and do their job carefully and meticulously so the final results are a thing of beauty. Don't let some early delays in the project with the window supplier or the concrete guy tempt you to "rush" the painters at the end because you are 3 weeks behind schedule. They truly despise that and it will show in their quality of work and you will regret it. Let them paint, at the pace they need to, in order to achieve excellence. It's not their fault some things happened prior to their arrival.

A good GC watches the progress each day, stays ahead of the progress by anticipating what items need to be ordered and keeps the supplies on the jobsite necessary to keep going. This is a daily process and you want to always look for ways to help the process, not be an obstruction to it. The goal is to have workers their every day until you are done. Sometimes, some work weeks will be 7 days. You will actually have guys willing to work Saturday and Sunday to get their work on your jobsite out of the way as they take on other projects when they get busier and busier. Use that to keep going when you can, but don't insist on a 7 day a week work schedule. Just know that it sometimes happens all by itself and you have to be there to keep things under control.

In the end, when it comes to scheduling, you can ball park a reasonable finish time, but nobody can ever predict the exact completion date on day one. There are too many variables and when you think about it, the nature of this kind of work is a series of sequential hand craftsmanship, which is not as easily predictable as an assembly line cranking out new minivans. Give yourself an intelligent time estimate broken down by trade and try to meet each mini completion date as it comes up in the chronology of the construction and keep guys there working and making progress each day. Remain vigilant each day as each trade makes progress and know that the entire construction process is a very fluid thing.

If you try to schedule each subcontractor for each trade for the next 30 days, you will be disappointed. You will have to constantly reschedule them. Instead, get the appropriate subcontractor in the sequence on the job site and keep the next subcontractor updated on their progress so they can show up when the one before them finishes. You are air traffic control, make sure the first jet takes off before you waive in the next jet in for a landing on the same runway...You get the idea. Keep the communication flowing. Sending out digital pictures of the jobsite progress to the subcontractors who will be arriving next on the jobsite is an easy way to alert them of what is going on. At times, they will see an opportunity to show up earlier to start the prep work because they "see" where you are at and can be comfortable getting started maybe a tad early. This is a very efficient way to keep the project going. Much of this is common sense and yet this facet baffles more people than you can imagine, even many GC's. I've listened to homeowners demand to know why the cabinets were not installed and I reply, "As I mentioned in our last 3 meetings and my last 6 emails to you before that over the last 3 weeks, you still need to pick a floor tile first so we can install it and *then* the cabinetry..."

Believe it or not, a week later, we'll have the same conversation. Why this is so complex, escapes me, but just about every homeowner starts to slouch a little right at the wrong time. They drag their feet on a selection and over think it, or simply fail to do their homework (actually shopping for the selection) and they go play golf instead. It happens and it causes delays.

This is a common cause of a delay. A selection is not made, in this case floor tile, because the homeowner procrastinates, which delays the tile being available to install and in so doing, delays the cabinetry installation and everything that follows the cabinetry installation. It's a domino effect, not an isolated issue detached and independent of the project. If you delay putting on your first pants leg, you will, in effect, delay putting on your other pants leg and therefore delay the entire process of getting dressed. Simple enough? I always think so, then continue to be amazed at what happens on a typical jobsite. Sometimes it's the counter tops. They try to pick a material (usually natural stone) and they can't make up their mind. So, as a result , I can't install the sinks or the faucets in the bathroom, or the kitchen, or the bar, or the butler's pantry, or the laundry room and so on...There is nothing to install them on! So, you wait...

Keep the subcontractors informed, keep the materials they need ready for them on the jobsite and make progress every working day. This is a daily routine of checking and rechecking each phase of the project to keep it going toward the finish line in an effective, disciplined fashion.

9   How do I check the quality of the work?

At first, this may seem daunting. How can you, if you are not familiar with all the nuances of quality workmanship at each phase of the project, check it for quality. Believe it or not, you are more capable than you imagine. Common sense is your primary tool. If something doesn't look right, ask about it. If you are satisfied with the answer, move on, if you think you are getting some "wool" pulled over your eyes, take a digital picture of it and send it to some people you consider knowledgeable. Ask a subcontractor who is involved with another trade what he thinks of the issue. Many are very knowledgeable about several other trades. Ask one of the local building inspectors what he thinks. Discuss it with your architect and send a digital picture of the issue. After all of those opinions, you should have a more confident assessment of what is going on and be much more educated about whatever issue caused you concern. You can even take it a step further and consult the internet and search for information concerning whatever issue puzzled you. If you start to hear a similar explanation from everyone, you can be confident you have the issue understood. If the building inspector considers the issue to be safe and properly built, chances are you have nothing to worry about. When in doubt, just ask. It shows a sense of responsibility to everyone, not ignorance. You're trying to do things right and when you demonstrate that sincerity, people respect that and help you out.

The good news is that your building permit paperwork from the building and zoning department will show you a list of inspections needed during specific intervals during the construction. The intention is for each critical stage of the construction to be examined before you can move on to the next stage. Make sure you are there for each inspection and the specific subcontractor is there whose work will be inspected that day. Listen to what the inspector says about the work. They are there to protect you from poor quality workmanship which can be potentially dangerous. Ask them their opinion of the overall jobsite when they show up to inspect something. Some of them are experts on any number of trades and can point out and educate you on many facets of the job you may be unfamiliar with. Don't be afraid to admit your ignorance about anything and to invite them to educate you because you simply want to make sure you do a good job and value their insights. They respect that far above individuals who think they know more than they do, which is plenty of the people they deal with each day. Most if not all inspectors will respond favorably to this and be more than willing to talk about anything you need a better understanding of. Many were former subcontractors and veterans of building and they will appreciate your forthright approach.

Always look at what is being done and ask questions during each stage of the project. That alone will result in deeper understandings of each component of the process. Be mindful of people's time though, as many workers on the jobsite are expected to accomplish a certain minimum level of progress each day as they try to meet their own deadlines. Believe it or not, the subcontractors have a financial incentive to work faster, not slower to get the work done as they are paid the same contract amount regardless. This is why it's important to have agreed upon, finalized contract totals before you start and not leave things open ended. Leaving things open ended means the subcontractors can just keep billing you until they are done with their work and you never know the final total until the end. This is referred to as a "time and material" contract and it is too open ended and a very dangerous scenario for you to control costs. You want finite contracts in writing. It's the only way to control costs. That way, there is incentive to knock out the work expeditiously and move on to the next jobsite. This type of contract generally results in a more professional and efficient approach to the work, because the subcontractor will not make any more money if the job takes longer to do, so he has incentive to get it done quickly and get paid.

Like we mentioned before, use common sense. If the floor does not feel level, rest a level on it and check it. If it's not level, address it. If the new walls being framed do not seem plumb, check them with a level. Periodically pull some measuring tape to make sure door openings are where they need to be as compared to the construction drawings and constantly look back and forth at the work and those drawings as the job progresses. You'll want your own set of drawings readily accessible at all times when you are on the jobsite and one for your home, when you have a question and need to check on something. Keep your jobsite construction drawing set in your vehicle when not in use, otherwise someone will borrow them and they may get misplaced on the jobsite.

If you spot something that concerns you and you know it's a mistake and the subcontractor is not on the jobsite that day, take a digital picture of it and send it in an email with an explanation of your concern. Make a list of issues of this nature and comb through the list each day until they are all resolved. Technology helps speed up the communication process involved in quality control, so like was said earlier, embrace useful technology like smart phones and digital camera features. They will help you keep a constructive dialogue going with each subcontractor which leads to improved quality on the road to achieving excellence.

If you see something done wrong, be sure to discuss it in an even tempered tone. Mistakes can happen, so you just have to respectfully address it and make sure the subcontractor follows up on your request. Most, if not all subcontractors respond well to a respectful tone when discussing mistakes, so use that tone and you will be glad you did. By using the techniques described earlier to identify the best subcontractors to hire for your project in the first place, you will have corrective conversations very, very rarely, if ever. That's the way you want it.

10   What are some issues to be aware of when making finish selections?

Eventually, in any new construction or renovation project, you have to make decisions on what you want in terms of what you "see." These are the finishes. They include, but are not limited to flooring, cabinetry, molding, doors, wainscoting, stairs, hand rails, plumbing fixtures, lighting fixtures, paint, wallpaper, you name it. If you can see it, it could be conceived of as a finish and you want to identify all of these before you ever start the job to avoid interruptions. That way, these items can be ordered and ready to be installed during project without delay. Not having this figured out ahead of time can be one of the biggest mistakes a homeowner can make during a renovation or new construction. There is not enough time to list all of the situations I have encountered where the homeowner was trying to decide on a selection during the construction phase and brought the job to a halt as a result. There is a specific chronology to the construction process and if you are delayed on one item, it delays all of the items after that. You can't skip around and keep going. There is a linear sequence of events which cannot be changed. If you get stuck because you're waiting on a decision, you're stopped cold. Period.

Think of it this way. You can't install a new window in your new room addition until the wall is built, right? You can't skip the wall part and just suspend the window in midair until the lumber for the wall shows up and you can catch up and build the wall around the floating window later. You *have to have* a wall before you have a window. That was obvious, so let me give you an example that may not be so obvious.

You're doing a master bathroom remodel and really going all out for a WOW scenario. That old plastic tub/shower combo from when the house was built is getting thrown away and you will have in its place a spectacular new shower with a beautiful custom tile design and high end fixtures and a custom glass door and opt to have a separate, stand alone, claw foot tub. Are you with me so far?

There are some other issues you are having done to your house as well and since you are having it done at the same time, it's a fairly large project and you just started. You have designed the shower size and layout with the architect, you have spent 2 weeks picking out the finest tile at the tile store. You picked out the tub and it's sitting in your garage waiting to be installed. You know exactly what the shower will look like from sketches....but...you are still capitulating on the plumbing fixtures for the shower and the tub and you have already started the project. This is a very awkward position to be in.

The old tub/shower has been ripped out, the walls for the new shower have been framed up, but are not covered yet, they are just suds at this point. The old floor tile has been ripped up and there is just the plywood left there. Everything is ready to keep going forward except for one major issue: The plumbing fixtures have not been picked out. You have been so busy with everything else, you have not finalized this yet and are still debating on which direction to go.

Bam. Everything has to stop now.

Why? Because until you choose the exact plumbing fixtures, it is impossible for the plumber to get his pipes in precise positions in the walls and floor to accommodate your specific fixtures. What if you wanted a rain shower head, he has to arrange a pipe for that. What if you have two individual volume controls for your hot and cold supplies? That is piped one way. What if you have a central temperature control and a separate volume control? That's piped another way. What if you want some body sprays? What if you want a hand held spray? What if you want a steam unit? All of these issues need specific answers before you close the walls up. All of the plumbing pipes need to be in precise positions before your shower walls can be closed tiled and there are specific valves that are installed behind the walls which are compatible with specific plumbing fixtures mounted on the surface of the tile. All of this has to be installed ahead of time and precisely located as you layout the position of the controls how you want them on your shower walls.

As far as the tub is concerned, you'll need to choose a filler which comes out of the wall or up from the floor. Either way, you'll need to choose it so the pipes behind the wall or under the floor can be positioned to accept the fixtures after the wall or floor is covered up.

So, until this is finalized, selected and the parts are on the jobsite, you cannot make any more progress. You are at a standstill until the fixtures are confirmed. What if you select one, but it will take 6 weeks to arrive from Germany? You stop working on this room and wait 6 weeks. It's that simple.

Can you see the importance of understanding the logistics of the process, so you don't ignorantly cost yourself a month and a half by not being prepared? This very issue happens more times than you can imagine. The homeowner falls in love with a fixture in a very elegant showroom somewhere and the salesperson takes their deposit and "orders" it and very intentionally avoids any definitive details about when the item will actually show up. Or, they give some vague and unrealistic date..."Maybe next week..." What do they care? They want the sale and the commission. If they harp on this lead time issue too much, you may go elsewhere and buy something more readily available. Besides, they can always blame the manufacturer for the delay. Are they all like this? No. But, does it happen? Absolutely! Every day.

This is a very real issue which merits slowing down on to understand more clearly. Some GC's could care less if you have a bunch of line items not picked out yet when you get started. Call these "selections." They know that if they can sign you up to a construction contract because you are in the frame of mind to get the project going, they will, regardless of if you are truly ready to start. They figure it's *your* problem. They'll shake your hand, take your money and know that if you stall out on them in the middle of the job because you didn't make an intelligent, readily available selection, they'll just go work on another job until you catch up. The goal for so many GC's is to sign you up and take your money, not to thoroughly prepare you. When you Think like a General Contractor, you understand how all the details are interconnected and how something seemingly minor can stop a project in its tracks. Therefore, it's not so minor is it?

Now, apply this "one thing directly affects another thing" concept to the subject of custom cabinetry and how it affects where you will have power outlets, internet jacks, cable TV jacks, heating vents and certain plumbing issues on top of that. You can see that if it takes 8 weeks to build your cabinets and you don't even have the drawings for the cabinets approved by the time you start construction, it's impossible to get the work done behind the walls (where the cabinets are to be installed) prior to their arrival. Lots of issues AFTER the walls and floors are closed affect the work that gets done BEFORE the walls and floors are closed.

You don't need the custom cabinets physically on the jobsite to start the work behind the walls and under the floor, you just need precise cabinet drawings with precise dimensions to get going. Knowing this will enable you to think ahead and not leave your project in limbo while you linger too long on the cabinetry design drawings without finalizing them. The day you start a construction job is the day you will need your cabinetry drawings finalized, even if the cabinets are not built yet. Those drawings will be used for critically important "behind the wall" work measurements which need to be done long before the cabinetry arrives. The exact location of power outlets, internet jacks, cable jacks, phone jacks, heating vents and such is always predicated upon where the cabinetry will eventually come to rest once it's installed. You have to get all of those issues in place first, so you do that by carefully examining the cabinetry drawings. The bottom line: Many homeowners are still making cabinetry design decisions after the construction begins and setting themselves up for a delay as a result. You want the cabinetry designs finalized before you start the construction. That's how you prevent unnecessary delays.

Consider this scenario. You have some under mount sink bowls coming in 2 weeks for the master bathroom double sink vanity. There is a $2,000 slab of natural stone being cut for the counter top. You can trust the sink bowl manufacture's website for the dimensions and shape of the oval under mount bowls and have the holes cut to match these dimensions. Or, you can wait for the bowls to arrive and use them to trace an exact size and shape for their holes in the counter top. Which is the safer choice? Which choice could ruin a $2,000 slab if it's wrong? Which requires some advance planning? Which is more likely to result in achieving excellence? You get the picture...

Let's talk about tile for a moment. The right tile can make any room look spectacular. The right combination of tile and tile design can make a room look beyond stunning. I have seen some real masterpieces over time and have a great respect for good tile designers. They are truly the difference makes in some rooms such as the master bathroom. However, I have seen some real swindlers too. Here is the way to tell the difference.

You want to do your master bathroom and really knock it out of the park in terms of elegance. You're changing the floor plan, making it bigger and you have architectural drawings to show that. The true professional tile designer will take your drawings and from those drawings create a floor design and any wall designs that are involved as well. Your shower will need 4 walls designed and possibly the ceiling too. Your air jet tub will need a tub deck design and a tub face design and some steps, if you want steps leading up the side of the tub face. The good designer will look at how your vanity and toilet are situated and the shower location and create a floor border which follows these contours with precise dimensions. That same designer will actually draw how this will look using the construction drawings you provided. They will also draw the walls of the shower individually. These wall designs are called "elevations." Any time you see a drawing showing the vertical side of something, it's an elevation. If you see a drawing of what you see looking down at something like a bird flying over it, it's a "plan" view.

A good tile designer will provide elevations and plan views to show where every last piece of tile goes and what the dimensions are for each feature. Is there tiled wainscoting? Is there a tiled backsplash ? Is the tub deck a slab of natural stone? Is the threshold for the shower the same stone material? Is the shower seat that same stone as well? Does this match the stone material for the vanity top? All of these questions are answered by a good tile designer. They calculate the total amount of tile you need (of each individually sized tile if there are several sized tiles needed) and the details in their drawings leave nothing to chance. Their drawings show exactly what you get and you end up with exactly what they drew. They typically have all of the material they show in the design and can show it to you. You can see the stone slabs they had in mind for your tub, shower and vanity issues and you can see everything before it's installed to make your decision before you sign off on the order.

Some tile companies have installers. Many do not, as the installation becomes a very delicate issue where many things can go wrong, some tile companies distance themselves from installation services as a result. Some grew tired of paying for installation mistakes and are content to just sell the material and be done with it. A good tile designer will spell everything out so that ANY installer you choose can work from their drawings and calculations. If you can find a competent tile company that designs and installs and carries everything you want, you have found a valuable combination. There will be cooperation and harmony and they will all work together to get the work done for you and it will be much easier to deal with them. One stop shopping can be a great thing when it comes to tile.

A bad tile company is something to be wary of and unfortunately they seem to exist just as frequently as the good tile companies. The soft economy is eliminating many more of the shady ones, but you still have to be cautious about those that remain.

The shady tile company "designers" will show you some pictures of beautiful designs, but are incapable of drawing them to conform to your specific master bathroom. This is a red flag. Their quantities are therefore, guesses, which may or may not be accurate. You don't want to get 75% through a tile job and run out of tile and have to wait 6 weeks for the next shipment which is coming from Italy...and does not quite match (the color of) the tile you have already installed. The bad tile companies don't care. They want your money (usually paid in advance or on delivery after a hefty deposit) and that's that. The rest of what happens will be on you. Even if they guessed right on the quantities, they may deliver tile that is 50% broken and unusable. Discuss this issue up front about their policy on returning broken tile. Examine all tile the moment it is delivered. You usually can't get very far with even a reputable tile company if you ask them for a refund 4 months after they deliver the tile. They assume it was damaged by some carelessness while the other subcontractors were renovating your house.

They will try to help you if their quantity guesses are not correct, but by then there could be some serious delay and color matching issues to contend with. In addition, they will have to "verbalize" the design to you, so you can "verbalize" it to the installer, if you hire a separate installer. This is a perfect recipe for mistakes. Discuss this right up front and insist on seeing some examples of their drawings. If you can't get tile design drawings, find another tile company. If they refuse to take back broken tile discovered upon delivery, find another tile company. If they refuse to provide a signed, notarized waiver upon final payment, find another tile company. If they demand an unreasonable percentage up front, find another tile company. You may find some material you love, but chances are, it's available at another tile company too.

The reason some of the shady companies thrive is because their prices are often lower than the reputable companies and they lure in the unsuspecting who think they just nailed a "bargain." They see the pretty showroom and like the charming people there, but they really are shortchanged without proper drawings and in jeopardy of some costly mistakes. Tile can be a complex matter made more complex by going to the wrong company. Do your homework on this one carefully and don't get enticed by some beautiful products in the window and the showroom. Try to understand how they do business and look for the warning signs and leave if you see them.

If you do find a reputable company and they require you to use your own installer, have that installer look over the drawings and the quantities before you commit to the order. It's common to order 10% more than the dimensions of your project for every type of tile needed as a precaution. Some designs warrant ordering 15% more. Your installer should look over their quantities as a second set of eyes to double check. In the end, the GC should know every dimension and do the math to make sure the quantities are right. Check and double check and check again. That's the path to achieving excellence.

Let's ponder the all important concept of cabinetry for a moment. If you're embarking on a high caliber renovation, you will likely engage a custom cabinetry company. Use all of the caution that you would use for working with a tile company and apply it to a cabinetry company. Also, used all of the suggestions about how to pick a cabinetry company to work with that you would use to choose any subcontractor. When you narrow it down, go see the products in person. There are differences and you should examine the quality closely, in person, to be sure. First off, look for a uniform finish among each cabinet. Does there seem to be a consistent color, or do there seem to be slight differences in shade as you move from cabinet to cabinet. If so, this is a bad sign to say the least. Look at the doors. Do they appear to line up nicely and close flush against the cabinet face? Most cabinet doors have hinges that adjust to make this possible, so the installer should have made these adjustments already. Do the hinges open and close with a solid, smooth motion? Do they have a soft, self close feature when you close the door nearly all the way? This is preferred in high end cabinets. They hold the doors closed when you want them closed. The truth is, I've seen some really expensive cabinets without this type of hinge. Not good, it's a corner that gets cut.

Do the drawers roll in and out smoothly with a nice soft self close feature similar to the doors? This is also preferred. Ask if the cabinetry company actually makes their own doors and drawer faces. Some don't and this is important. If they simply make the cabinet boxes, which is the easiest part of the job, then farm out the doors to a separate company, there may be some longer lead times to build the cabinets and there may be some longer times you will have to wait for a replacement if there are any items that show up damaged upon delivery. If possible, it is preferable to work with a company who makes all of the components (besides hinges and hardware) themselves. This gives you a better turnaround time if there is something that needs to be remade and frankly more control over the entire process as well.

Painted cabinets are generally more expensive than stained cabinets, so look for examples of their painted cabinets and study the paint. Is it smooth, evenly toned and seemingly the same thickness all over?

This is a nice paint job. If you see rough spots that look like someone painted over a section that was not sanded properly or if you see drips or uneven color tones, this is never acceptable, no matter the "bargain" price you may have struck.

Make sure the drawings for the cabinets have a top view and elevation views full of measurements and double check the measurements with your tape measure on the jobsite. Some companies do so much business, they transpose some measurements with other clients and the next thing you know, you have a custom entertainment center being delivered and it's a foot too wide for the space, which is a disaster. Always double check the cabinetry drawings in the field to see if they make sense. Some GC's go the extra step of using blue painter's tape to map out where a cabinet is going to make sure it's perfectly measured. You're never wrong to check measurements over and over. People can make mistakes and you have to anticipate that and save yourself the agony of having something remade. A good GC checks everyone's work when it comes to measurements for custom made items. He is the last resort in terms of a safety net for any errors.

When the cabinet drawings are done, long before the cabinets are delivered, a copy of the drawings, which has been thoroughly checked by you, goes to the plumber, electrician, HVAC tech and anyone else who needs to get something done behind the wall or in the floor or ceiling that will be impacted by the cabinetry. They will use those drawings to get their measurements calculated to make sure all the pipes, power outlets, jacks, switches, heating vents and so forth are in place and ready when the cabinets are installed.

Once the cabinets are installed, in the case of lower cabinets in a kitchen, a butler's pantry, a bathroom vanity or a bar, the countertop guys can come in and measure the cabinets in their final installed positions. These measurements are used to cut (fabricate) the countertop to the exact size necessary to fit the cabinet. The countertop guys should never, ever use the cabinetry drawings for this measurement. Their measurements need to be perfectly precise and based on the precise measurements of the existing conditions for that specific cabinet, with no exceptions. Also, the GC should never relay measurements to the countertop fabricator for the purpose of cutting any slabs for countertops. If there are any measurement mistake issues whatsoever, they should fall on the shoulders of the fabricator. If he messes up, he needs to buy another slab of material and start over. He should never be able to say he was "given the wrong measurement" by the GC. You may never encounter this situation, but if you do work with a fabricator who is too lazy to come out and take a field measurement for this purpose and wants you to, insist that he comes out. It's that important.

11   What about appliances?

Appliances are both complex and easy. The complex part is what you want and what your budget will support. Take your time on this one. There are some very expensive choices out there and they often do little more than their significantly cheaper rivals. Only you can determine which caliber of appliance makes sense for you, but if you need help determining that, start with your architect. You can also ask a realtor or your interior designer if you work with one. Knowing the caliber of appliances in your neighborhood and your caliber home is important. If you are about to embark on a significant makeover, you don't want to come up short in this category. It just doesn't look right.

About the only way to save on the really top of the line brands is to buy the "about to be discontinued" model which they start discounting just prior to the arrival of the new models. A candid discussion with your sales representative will help make your intentions clear. Also, make sure when you settle on what you want, that you price it against at least one other local retailer. As a final note, price it against an internet retailer and see who wants your business the most.

After negotiating them all down to the last nickel, ask who will include an extended warranty, installation and delivery. Make that the deal maker or breaker. Your tax is an issue as well. Always examine the deal with all of its parts. Sometimes, in order to clinch a deal, you may even get one appliance for $10 as part of a package. I've seen that. A $500 microwave was thrown in for $10 to make the deal work. Ask for it. Be polite, but be clear. Once you settle on your choices, it's an apples to apples comparison among the retailers, so you have no allegiance to who you buy them from. Remind them of that, but be polite. These are commodities, literally the same item no matter who sells it to you, so it's a matter of who really wants to grant you the best deal. It's that simple.

When it comes to your appliances, do your homework on what you want first. Don't wander into a gorgeous showroom and get dazzled. Spend some time researching the brands you are considering and be cautious when you enter the showrooms and start chatting with a highly trained salesman. Some are exceptionally skilled at filling your head with information that is highly misleading. I know, I've seen some of these sleight of hand scenarios before.

I knew a homeowner who stopped into a local appliance store and was intercepted by one of their most skilled salesmen. They took hours picking out a whole slew of items for his house and when the grand total was generated it was a very large number. Buried among dozens of line items was a charge for over $60,000 for some wiring. The wiring in the bid was similar to wiring normally costing around $1,200. However, this wiring was portrayed as the level of quality absolutely needed to serve the items he was buying and he was lead to believe he would notice a significant quality difference if he used anything other than this specific wiring. He eventually took his business elsewhere and saved over $100,000 in doing so for the exact same list of items and never missed a beat in quality or performance. Why? He didn't roll over and believe every word of their story and made the effort to get educated on the wiring. He checked with me and some other experts and learned this story was far from legitimate and simply a ploy to generate over $58,000 in additional profit. Retailers can be very shrewd in their efforts to sell you something, especially if it's a very technical product. They make a technical case for consulting you toward a certain package and you lack the expertise to spot any misrepresentations in their story and they know it.

There are some extremely complex details to consider when sorting through the high end appliance maze. Take the time to educate yourself and be prepared before you engage a salesperson. When it comes to home theater systems, this is even more important.

Technology is changing very rapidly and in some cases reducing the cost of items that will really serve you well for years to come. Do your homework first. If you run out to the store without spending some time on your computer researching quality reviews, technology changes and products soon to be released, it can be a costly mistake. Do you know the primary differences between plasma and LCD or LCD/LED TV's? If you don't, some of the gaming equipment you intend to connect it to it may start to permanently deteriorate the picture quality from day one. Ouch. (Hint: Go with the LCD...)

Figure out the caliber of appliances commensurate with your house, identify the model you should buy, negotiate the price and other issues like installation and enjoy your bargain. That's Thinking like a General Contractor.

12 What if I just want to hire a General Contractor? How do I pick the right one and not get taken for a ride?

If I could do nothing more than get this concept across to homeowners, the villains out there would be out of business in a week and you would be left with just the sensational General Contractors delivering quality work at a fair price. New construction and renovation would boom as people would not fear it, they would enjoy it and relish the opportunity to get a project going. Countless foreclosed homes would get snapped up, whipped back into shape and enjoyed once again. New houses would start popping up all over. Neighborhoods would appreciate in value as people truly invested in their homes. Genuine value would be created, not just money spent and gone forever. That being said, let's ponder how to pick the right GC to get the job done in a professional manner and not crush your checkbook by the time you're done.

Now that you understand more of the mindset of a competent GC, it will be more difficult to be mislead into hiring an incompetent one. There are a few more important issues to cover, to protect you from getting really set up and taken for a lot of money, so we'll get into some of those tactics as well.

After you have checked in with the best sources for names of competent General Contractors, like your friends and the local building and zoning department and your architect, there are some specific ways to filter down to your best choice. Start with the short list of names you generated by those methods first. Call each one and ask if they have current liability and worker's compensation insurance and to please fax the certificate to you. The ones who manage to fax you a certificate successfully should get another call back from you.

When you call them back, ask a simple question: "Can I see your finished work in person?"

Notice that you are not going to ask for pictures. How do you know it's his work? Notice that you did not ask for references. How do you know the 4 phone numbers and names he provides are not his next door neighbor, his aunt and two old high school friends? You really don't do you--and believe me, that stunt gets pulled out there.

You want to visit and see the work in person, put your hands on it, inspect it up close and really study the attention to detail of every feature. As a result of being there, you will likely have to meet the homeowner who had the work done. This is key. Look into their eyes and ask how they liked the GC. Ask an open ended question like that and observe how they react. Do they seem genuinely impressed by the guy or does this seem like an uncomfortable question? Their eyes will tell you and your gut will confirm it. Then, be more specific. Was the budget met? Exceeded? Why or why not? Was it done on time? Were there any work stoppages? How were the subcontractors--did they seem competent? How was the experience? Was the GC accessible? Here each day? Easy to communicate with? Did he handle changes well? Are you pleased overall? Do you think you added value to your home? Do you like how it turned out and have there been any problems since finishing? Did the GC address them promptly? Have you recommended the GC to anyone since you started working with him?

These types of questions, asked face to face while personally examining the workmanship, will flush out any issues. If your gut tells you something awful went on between the GC and the client, but nobody's coming right out and saying it, trust your gut. If you see some flaws in the workmanship, trust your eyes. You can only get this caliber of evaluation by going to their client's house. There is no substitute for this. None. This is the absolute gold standard test of a

GC's competence. You can skip this part if you like, but you are assuming an awful lot about a GC's competence by other people's opinions, not your own, which is the only opinion that counts.

As a GC, I can't *wait* for people to see my work. The work speaks for itself, but so do my clients and that's the only way to conclude a job. When my clients are genuinely impressed and speak sincerely about my work, that feels great and it helps potential clients know that they can trust my competence. It's just good business to do a good job because people will speak highly of you with their peers and your potential clients. You can never lose sight of that as a GC. The GC to avoid is the one who just looks toward the next client and can't wait to be done with the current client and doesn't really care about the current one moments after they sign the contract. The only way to thoroughly uncover this is to look the current or former client in the eye when you ask your due diligence questions. The GC's that pass this vetting process should be allowed to submit a bid to you for the project.

Make sure that your scope of work is clearly expressed in architectural drawings and / or a sheet listing all of the items you wish to have the GC obtain bids for. You want to standardize your scope of work so that each GC understands exactly what you want and their bids will be genuine apples to apples comparisons. Taking it a step further, you could list each item on a vertical column on a spreadsheet and email that to each GC. Then you would get an exact, apples to apples comparison and see the differences immediately line by line and be able to ask questions.

As an aside, I met a very accomplished, high ranking executive in a very prestigious company who asked me to bid the construction of his sizable, newly designed house. He was very intelligent and really took the time to try to understand the bidding process. He even went to the trouble of creating his own personal spreadsheet which he passed out to each GC so he could standardize the bidding process. I thought that, in theory, was brilliant.

It was the first time I had ever seen someone do that and I sincerely respected his intensions. However, he was also somewhat misguided in his understanding of the construction bidding process and he assumed that by forcing each GC to "disclose" all sorts of separate line items, he would somehow expose the riff raff out there and get everyone to tip their hand. He thought this would be a very clever high pressure transparency drill for all of us to go through and it would somehow separate the good GC's from the bad ones.

He handed me the spreadsheet with the wry smile of a riverboat gambler laying down a royal flush at the card table . I think his spreadsheet had about 30 line items and he had a demeanor of "gotcha now!" I explained that I would be happy to accommodate him, but that my bidding spreadsheet typically disclosed much more detail and I showed him an example of one I had with me. There were over 340 line items of detail. He was silent. His effort to trap everyone and make them disclose things clearly fell way, way short. I actually had to bid the house out the proper way with a proper spreadsheet, then cram the information into his limited line item spreadsheet and combine issues together to conform to his format. This made the information we all provided for him much less useful and clear. For example, if you combine all the "plumbing fixtures" for 12 different rooms and only list a total plumbing fixture cost, how can you distinguish what dollar amount is going into the master bathroom and what is going into the kitchen and make decisions from there? The right way to do a spreadsheet is to break it down room by room and clarify all of those details so you know exactly what you are getting in each room. His spreadsheet did not accommodate this and so his strategy, I'm sure, only made him more confused. I give him and "A" for effort, but a "D" in execution because he just didn't have a grip on the ability to Think like a General Contractor.

The bottom line: Make sure you define your scope of work as clearly as possible and take the time to categorize it by each room you are renovating with a complete list of the labor and materials you will need for each room. Then meet each GC on the jobsite and walk it with them and hand them the list and answer any questions they have. They may need to meet some of their subcontractors at your home to look things over as they bid out the job. Accommodate this, it's normal and necessary. Once you receive their bids, make the time to visit with them in person and review the bids with them line by line.

Ask questions, listen, observe how they carry themselves and if they are good communicators. It's a job interview. Literally. You are the boss. Let the most talented candidate shine through and make your choice for you. In the unlikely event that they are all equal in your mind and all priced equally, ask about the time frames for completion and any "movement" on cost and let those criteria influence your final choice. Notice I did not say, "Hire the cheapest one." If all things were standardized and equal, that would be a logical conclusion. It never is, so you have to make some judgment calls, but you will have narrowed it down to the most qualified candidates by now and that in itself is an enormous advantage.

If there are price differences, identify where they are and ask why. Always try to understand the underlying reason for any price differences. In so doing, you may uncover an issue that you are willing to pay more for that the others have left out. One GC, for example, may have assumed that you wanted a natural stone counter top (like marble or granite) for your master vanity and he was correct. The others may have assumed that a "cultured" or "engineered" (man-made) countertop was acceptable and may have a cheaper price in that line item for their bids as a result. You wanted the natural stone, so make sure everyone knows that up front. It's a scope of work detail that should not be omitted.

Now, you've standardized the scope of work on a spreadsheet and you have architectural drawings too. Pass these out through email to save yourself some printing costs. At the bidding stage, a GC can work off of an emailed file of your construction drawings. That's all he needs and if you email it to him, it makes it easier on him to forward to his subcontractors. Send that to him along with your spreadsheet and let him look it over then bring it to your jobsite to go over any questions.

Hint: A good smart phone has the ability to take a picture of your full size (36" wide x 24" tall) construction drawings and you can download it to your PC (or Mac) and create a picture file with that digital image. You can also just email the picture image right from your smart phone . Simple. Easy. Fast.

Now, as the bids start to roll in, insist that they correlate with the way you set up your scope of work spreadsheet. This will help keep everything clear and organized. The GC's will simply use your spreadsheet and plug in the costs. The rest will figure something out...

For the sake of illustration, let's pretend we're doing a kitchen makeover and you have 3 GC's bidding that are all superb. Now, it's just a matter of cost, which can involve a whole new level of shell games, so buckle up, it's about to get a little bumpy. The existing kitchen flat ceiling will be raised for a tray ceiling with some cove lighting. You'll need the bids for these items and you would also provide the drawings for the way the kitchen will look when you're done. It shows a plan view and four elevations, one for each wall. For the purpose of making this a more simple spreadsheet with some space limitations in this format, I have combined some "labor and material" situations on a few line items. You would want that separated. I combined them to shorten the list. The list of line items you need bids for could look like this:

demolition

lumber
insulation
1 brand "x" dishwasher
1 brand "x" cook top
1 brand "x" oven
1 brand "x" refrigerator
1 brand "x" microwave
1 brand "x" exhaust hood
plumbing fixtures
light fixtures
under cabinet lighting
cove lighting
4 switches
6 receptacles
1 TV / internet jack
cabinetry
cabinetry hardware (brushed nickel)
countertop (granite material and labor)
backsplash (porcelain tile material and labor)
drywall (labor and material)
hardwood flooring (labor and material)
painting (labor and material)
1 interior French door 30" x 6'-8"
French door hardware (brushed nickel)
crown, casing, base molding
carpentry framing labor
trim carpentry labor
electrician (labor and material for wiring)
plumber (labor and material for pipes)
dumpster
portable toilet
grand total of labor and material

General Contractor fee (percentage)
building permit
grand total

For the purpose of illustration, on the following pages, I have made up some names for some fictitious General Contracting companies and for some fictitious subcontractors. They are by no means meant to represent any real companies. This bid below is what you could conceivably get as one of your bids. Let's call this bid ACME GENERAL CONTRACTING.

ACME GENERAL CONTRACTING

$700.00	demolition
$500.00	lumber
$250.00	insulation
$850.00	1 brand "x" dishwasher
$3,500.00	1 brand "x" cook top
$4,950.00	1 brand "x" oven
$7,580.00	1 brand "x" refrigerator
$400.00	1 brand "x" microwave
$550.00	1 brand "x" exhaust hood
$1,600.00	plumbing fixtures
$1,650.00	light fixtures
$475.00	under cabinet lighting
$1,200.00	cove lighting
$400.00	4 switches
$300.00	6 receptacles
$50.00	1 TV / internet jack
$29,650.00	cabinetry
$1,250.00	cabinetry hardware (brushed nickel)
$5,850.00	countertop (granite material and labor)
$1,850.00	backsplash (porcelain tile material and labor)
$750.00	drywall (labor and material)
$2,600.00	hardwood flooring (labor and material)
$1,350.00	painting (labor and material)
$150.00	1 interior French door 30" x 6'-8"
$35.00	French door hardware (brushed nickel)
$1,100.00	crown, casing, base molding
$1,200.00	carpentry framing labor
$2,850.00	trim carpentry labor
$2,600.00	electrician (labor and material for wiring)

$3,100.00	plumber (labor and material for pipes)
$850.00	dumpster
$300.00	portable toilet
$80,440.00	grand total of labor and material
$7,239.60	General Contractor fee 9%
$1,500.00	building permit
$89,179.60	grand total

From the looks of this, ACME GENERAL CONTRACTING will make 9% of the total labor and materials which amounts to $7,176.60 right? Every line item has a cost and there are no unaccounted for line items, so this is a straightforward bid, right? All quality issues being equal, if the other GC bids came in for much higher fee percentages like 15% or 18%, you would pick ACME GENERAL CONTRACTING at 9%, right?

Notice that they do not reveal who their subcontractors are. If you agree to pay ACME GENERAL CONTRACTING and they in turn, pay the subcontractors, there could be a whole layer of profit for them that you are not privy to, because you don't know the real total cost of each subcontractor on each line item. You just know the cost which the GC shows you, which could be substantially more than his real cost.

In this example, if he expects you to pay him first and then he pays the subcontractors, it's not exactly clear if these numbers are accurate, or if the real subcontractor bids are in fact, substantially less than these numbers. If that is the case, he could easily be making an extra $12,000 or $13,000 profit that you are not privy to---giving him more like a 25% fee, not a modest 9% fee which he is implying by this spreadsheet. Can you see the sleight of hand here? This GC might be the most expensive of them all when you consider his "real" total profit, but it's camouflaged by that 9% "fee" at the bottom of his spreadsheet which he wants you to fixate on, which does not account for the extra profit he makes on some of the other line items. You have no way of knowing that hidden profit number and that's exactly the way he wants it. He wants you to think he's making 9% and he's the lowest price GC you have a bid from. In reality, he might be the GC with the highest fee and you end up with some substandard subcontractors to help him accomplish this.

So how do you protect yourself from this? You ask to see the contracts for the subcontractors and you make it clear you want full disclosure. You need to be polite about it and you need to pay a reasonable profit to any GC, but you also have a right to know what they are truly charging and not accept any shell game tactics. This is a delicate matter prior to hiring the GC as he will not want to disclose his subcontractor's identities to you prior to being hired. This is a legitimate proprietary matter for GC's, but you can make it clear you want to see that the contracts match the spreadsheet he is handing you and you will ultimately want to see all of the subcontractor contracts after you come to terms and hire him. You can also insist that he show you a version of the spreadsheet with the subcontractor's company names, although he does not need to leave that document with you until you sign up with him. Also, make it clear that if you determine that the subcontractor's actual contracts at any time do not reflect the contract totals that you see on his spreadsheet, he will be fired. Put that addendum in his contract and have him agree to it and initial it. If he is above board, this should not be an issue. Also, make it clear that you will be paying the subcontractors with checks made directly out to them individually and that you expect signed notarized lien waivers every time you make a payment. Any fees owed to the GC will be by a check to them separately. This cuts off all possible opportunities for shell game tactics and misrepresentations of contracts and such.

As you communicate your requirements to do business, use your gut. The GC's who respond easily to these requests are preferable to do business with over the ones who look like they're getting seasick when you set this tone. Shady people have a tendency get very uncomfortable when you start exposing their tactics. Look them in the eye. It likely won't be hard to pick the honest, competent GC once you do.

If you simply take the GC's spreadsheet at face value and believe every contract number on it and agree to pay him, so he can in turn pay the subcontractors, can you see the obvious incentive for the GC to hire some cheaper and cheaper subcontractors to increase his hidden profit in this way? Can you see how that may affect the quality of the work? Can you see how you should also insist that each subcontractor who works on your job to provide a certificate of insurance for liability and worker's comp? You can do this, you know, it's your job and you have the right to make the rules. All you are doing is eliminating opportunities for any tactics that can work against you. You can never be too careful these days. Even competent GC's in a soft economy can do some things out of financial desperation. Protect yourself. You are the only one who can. You have a right to choose to do business with people in an open, fair manner.

This next one is a little more tricky. You'll notice that the GC fee is 15%, which is higher than the GC fee for ACME GENERAL CONTRACTIING but the overall cost is considerably lower. So, this might be the best GC to hire, right!! ?? Look at the grand total: $74,801.00, that's over $13,000 cheaper than ACME GENERAL CONTRACTING and the bottom line is the bottom line right? It sure makes the SMITH JONES CONSTRUCTION bid a hard offer to pass up, doesn't it?

SMITH JONES CONSTRUCTION

$700	demolition
$500.00	lumber
$250.00	insulation
$850.00	1 brand "x" dishwasher
$3,500.00	1 brand "x" cook top
$4,950.00	1 brand "x" oven
$7,580.00	1 brand "x" refrigerator
$400.00	1 brand "x" microwave
$550.00	1 brand "x" exhaust hood
$1,600.00	plumbing fixtures
$1,650.00	light fixtures
$475.00	under cabinet lighting
$1,200.00	cove lighting
$400.00	4 switches
$300.00	6 receptacles
$50.00	1 TV / internet jack
$17,500.00	cabinetry (allowance)
$1,250.00	cabinetry hardware (brushed nickel)
$2,000.00	countertop (granite material and labor) (allowance)
$1,850.00	backsplash (porcelain tile material and labor)
$750.00	drywall (labor and material)
$2,600.00	hardwood flooring (labor and material)
$1,350.00	painting (labor and material)
$150.00	1 interior French door 30" x 6'-8"
$35.00	French door hardware (brushed nickel)
$1,100.00	crown, casing, base molding
$1,200.00	carpentry framing labor
$2,850.00	trim carpentry labor
$2,600.00	electrician (labor and material for wiring)
$3,100.00	plumber (labor and material for pipes)
$850.00	dumpster
$300.00	portable toilet
$64,440.00	grand total of labor and material
$9,666.00	General Contractor fee 15%

$1,500.00   building permit
$75,606.00   grand total

Look closer. How is the total so much cheaper? Look at the line item for cabinetry and countertop. The term "allowance" is there. This is an important and *dangerous* term. It means "guesstimate," not official, finalized bid. When a line item is designated an allowance, it does not have a finite contract associated with it. It means this figure is just a guess, subject to being revised once a real bid number is inserted. It also means that this line item could grow substantially larger once the contract for this line item is finalized. Can you see that by showing what looks to be a legitimate spreadsheet with a number on each line item, this total bid could grow by thousands of dollars for these two line items and the $75,606.00 grand total could conceivably turn into well over $100,000 in a hurry if the cabinets finally come in for $39,000 when the dust settles and the countertop comes in at $6,000. Can you see how showing someone a total project cost of $75,606.00 might make them more likely to sign a contract than showing them a $100,000 total? The GC will shrug his shoulders and inform you that the cabinets and countertop "went over budget" as if it was some sort of a surprise to him.

In reality, he purposely put an unrealistically low "allowance" number in those two line items and slid it in front of you knowing that you would ignore his higher fee of 15% and fixate on the artificially low grand total of $75,606.00. You get suckered and he gets the contract and is also very protected because he will call the two line items "allowance" figures, so they could change dramatically once the final contract for that line item is determined. The real numbers for these lines items will be inserted for these two line items, conveniently, *after* the contract is signed. They will then be followed by two "change orders" which will simply state "adjustment to reflect actual bid cost." This all looks legitimate, but is very much calculated to mislead. Low balling some line items with "allowances" to create an artificially low grand total is a tactic, so be cautious when someone slides a spreadsheet in front of you. Ask if all of the line items are "hard" numbers, which means derived from actual bids. Then, ask if you can see the bids. If the GC turns pale...that's a bad sign. Never believe a spreadsheet is full of 100% legitimate numbers. You have to drill down and confirm that. The spreadsheet is a tool often used more to get you to commit to a construction contract, than to express complete transparency. Because of that, you have to be extremely cautious about every line item of information in the spreadsheet and question its legitimacy. The only way to confirm that 100% is if the number matches a bid, which you can look at. Could you ask for that? Why wouldn't you? Every day, people walk into new car dealerships with a print out of the invoice for the car they really want in one hand and the keys to their current car in their other hand. That's where they *start* to negotiate. I say, everyone should do the same when it comes to negotiating with their GC. Know the "invoice" number when you are studying the costs. In this case, "invoice" means the subcontractor contract numbers. An honest GC will not have a problem with this.

This is one of the reasons some projects go so far over budget. They were never intended to stay on budget from the start! The budget was unrealistic, so a crafty GC strategically loaded spreadsheet with "allowances" which are just ticking time bombs that go off when the real prices are finalized and come into focus. Many projects that go way over budget simply started out as a misleading spreadsheet that a homeowner didn't fully understand. They might have had an unrealistic budget for their goals to begin with, which is not uncommon. Then, they assumed that every time they see a column of line items with prices next to them that those prices have some sort of inherent truthfulness and accuracy and cannot be manipulated at the discretion of the GC.

It would be pure ignorance to think this and you have to insist on disclosure and accuracy at every turn in the process. If you don't, that nice friendly GC in the old faded baseball cap who drives the big 4 wheel drive truck with his name pasted all over it will rob you blind while showing you pictures of his son's little league team. CEO's, Presidents, successful entrepreneurs, doctors, lawyers and bankers read these kinds of spreadsheets each day and get duped. These are smart people and they still get taken for a ride when it comes to building or improving their home.

How do you protect yourself from this?

1. You insist on getting every single line item bid out with a hard, black and white, finite contract number--no allowances allowed.

2. You insist on full disclosure so you know exactly how much each subcontractor's contract is and that includes the General Contractor as well. You want to know clearly and plainly where your money is going. There is nothing wrong with paying someone a profit. It's fair to insist on knowing exactly what that profit is and not to be mislead.

3. You make it clear that the GC will not be paid in order to distribute the money to the subcontractors. That places him in the middle of the transaction and creates opportunities for a long list of things you want to avoid. You insist on paying the subcontractors and the GC every 30 days directly with separate, individual checks according to the percentage of work that was done, in exchange for signed, notarized lien waivers.

4. You demonstrate that you are knowledgeable, observant, willing to pay a fair wage for an honest effort, capable of understanding the details of the construction process, willing to be helpful in the effort and eager to achieve excellence in every respect. If that is accomplished, you make it clear that you are willing to be a solid reference for the GC to anyone considering him for their project.

The following is what a legitimate, full disclosure spreadsheet should look like:

BEST BUILDERS

$700.00	jack's carpentry	demolition
$500.00	hanks lumber company	lumber
$250.00	house of insulation	insulation
$850.00	appliance brothers	1 brand "x" dishwasher
$3,500.00	appliance brothers	1 brand "x" cook top
$4,950.00	appliance brothers	1 brand "x" oven
$7,580.00	appliance brothers	1 brand "x" refrigerator
$400.00	appliance brothers	1 brand "x" microwave
$550.00	appliance brothers	1 brand "x" exhaust hood
$1,600.00	the plumbing depot	plumbing fixtures
$1,650.00	smith lighting company	light fixtures
$475.00	smith lighting company	under cabinet lighting
$1,200.00	smith lighting company	cove lighting
$400.00	electrical supply house	4 switches
$300.00	electrical supply house	6 receptacles
$50.00	electrical supply house	1 TV / internet jack
$29,650.00	cabinets are us	cabinetry
$1,250.00	cabinets are us	cabinetry hardware (brushed nickel)
$5,850.00	frank's stone and tile	countertop (granite material and labor)
$1,850.00	frank's stone and tile	backsplash (tile material and labor)
$750.00	drywall experts	drywall (labor and material)
$2,600.00	joe's flooring company	hardwood flooring (labor and material)
$1,350.00	rainbow of colors painting	painting (labor and material)
$150.00	hanks lumber company	1 interior French door 30" x 6'-8"
$35.00	hanks lumber company	French door hardware (brushed nickel)

$1,100.00	hanks lumber company	crown, casing, base molding
$1,200.00	jack's carpentry	carpentry framing labor
$2,850.00	gunter trim carpenters	trim carpentry labor
$2,600.00	blue jay electric	electrician (labor and material for wiring)
$3,100.00	jones plumbing and sewer	plumber (labor and material for pipes)
$850.00	debris be gone	dumpster
$300.00	sanitation experts	portable toilet
$80,440.00		grand total of labor and material
$14,479.20	Best Builders	General Contractor fee 18%
$1,500.00	building and zoning dept	building permit
$96,419.20		grand total

This bid from BEST BUILDERS represents the most honest, straightforward bid of them all. It is the highest bid, but it is the most honest and safest bid. First of all, it shows a legitimate starting point to work from--the truth. You have all the money clearly identified for the actual subcontractors and are conceivably getting top notch subcontractors as a result. There are no hidden profits to the GC which are not disclosed and cheaper, inferior subcontractors used to accomplish this. Second of all, you know exactly, to the penny, what the GC is making. This is an honest, disclosed, reasonable number and one you can live with.

If you proceed with this GC and get started, you have eliminated every possible pre-construction price surprise, because you have a spreadsheet with finite bids without any guesstimates or allowances. The only surprises that can occur from this point forward is what could happen when your walls are opened up and the floor is opened up.

That's when you check for any unsafe items that need addressing like damaged, hazardous wiring from when the home was built that needs to be updated and made safe or some floor joists which split years ago which could use some shoring up. Otherwise, you have defined as many of the cost variables as you could, prior to starting the construction. That's the way you want it.

In the last example, the GC makes about $14,000 and you get top notch subcontractors. In the first example, the GC could ultimately make $20,000 or more as the result of collecting money from you and paying the cheapest subcontractors he can find to do the work, which often means corners are cut and workmanship is inconsistent and sometimes unacceptable. In the middle example, SMITH JONES CONSTRUCTION, the guy bidding $75,606, you will be shocked to find the two most expensive items on the spreadsheet were intentionally represented by lower than realistic "guesstimate" numbers. Why? Because it works. It lowers the bottom line number and that baits the homeowner. As an aside, this GC might not have tagged the line items with the term "allowance." He might even be more subtle and just *verbalize* that to you in passing and when the issue comes up during the construction process, he could say "We talked about that being just an allowance, remember? Here is the actual contract number for that line item, now that I have it from the cabinetry company. Here you go, just sign this right here."

KA CHING!!!!! Bam! Your project just went up $20,000 in the blink of an eye.

You can be that SMITH JONES CONSTRUCTION will re-calculate the new grand total once that gets ironed out and then take their 15% fee on the *new total*, which will drive their fee right up as well. Think of this as a little delayed reaction Trojan Horse effect on your wallet which conveniently only materializes *after* you sign the contract. You'll be falsely confident that because you're looking at an official looking spreadsheet document that all of the prices are locked in and final and can't change. Two of the prices are intentionally not final in this example and they are strategically buried among the rest. Imagine if a whole series of prices were hidden like this, among firm prices, what the financial ramifications would be over the course of the construction. Now you understand one of the major reasons that projects "unexplainably" go way over in cost. The tiny bottom line total is an irresistible bait for the trap and highly intelligent people fall for this trick every day. Why? Because they don't Think like a General Contractor and understand a legitimate spreadsheet and simply see through this tactic.

You get what you pay for, as the saying goes. If you hire a shady GC, you will pay that GC handsomely, but not the subcontractors who will ultimately do the work. Where do you want your money going, to the guys actually building your kitchen or the guy who hired them?

There is no reason you can't ask everyone to abide by your rules when it comes to bidding your project and once you gather the spreadsheets from each GC and they look the way you want them to, there is no reason not to ask if they can do even *better* on the price. You just want everyone on the same page when it comes to how you conduct business and that page is honesty and full disclosure, not shell games and misdirection.

Does this sound unsettling? It should. This kind of thing happens every day. People emerge from their private jet all giddy and plop into the leather back seat of a polished limousine to sip absurdly expensive champagne. They declare triumphant toasts to themselves for their unmatched negotiating skills in relentlessly reducing the fee percentage for the GC building their brand new dream house with a brilliantly timed "take it or leave it" ultimatum. Little do they know, that's exactly how it was planned and they're simply just another victim of some very subtle tactics which will cost them dearly on several levels, while substantially enriching the GC. They have an MBA and run a huge publicly traded company and the GC never finished high school. Isn't life just laughably ironic sometimes? Knowledge is power, as they say. Too often, a slick GC is the only one in the room with the most important knowledge and he would like to keep it that way. I think the playing field should be level and only the GC's who can deliver top quality for a fair and honestly stated price should win, not the one who can play the best shell game. Too often, slimy tactics win over the client when their ignorance is so susceptible to it.

The GC who connects with you honestly on this issue is the one you should go with, all other issues being equal. That's the GC who is not uncomfortable being transparent and shows you exactly how the money is distributed and exactly what his fees will be and those of his subcontractors with complete disclosure. An open, honest GC is your best GC when everything else is equal in terms of quality. You won't likely get this level of openness, you'll have to ask for it. Those that respond well have nothing to hide. If you can Think like a General Contractor, you will be all that much closer to hiring the right one.

Honest pricing aside, make sure you have a discussion with the GC you want to hire about his supervision philosophy. Will he be there personally every day? Some guys sign you up and send in a flunky to check on things most of the time, or they consider one of the carpenters on the job a surrogate supervisor. That's a quality problem waiting to happen. You can't concentrate on being a productive, competent carpenter while managing the efforts of several other trades simultaneously. There is too much concentration and focus needed for each job. Both efforts will suffer if you try to be both. You can only be effective at one or the other, a carpenter or a project manager. Some GC's like to alleviate their need to be on the jobsite daily by relying on this technique. This is a recipe for issues to slip through the cracks. You want a guy there every day, diligently watching the progress and combing through the site every day. They need to constantly be searching for problems before they happen and also facilitating the needs of every subcontractor on the project to continue forward each day with uninterrupted momentum. Period. No exceptions. When you do your due diligence on the GC, make sure you uncover if he was on the jobsite every day and ask him if he intends to be on your jobsite every day. If he blinks, this is a red flag, so insist that he be there and write that in the contract if you have to, to make sure he is.

13   What are some common mistakes to avoid on the road to achieving excellence?

The road to successful results passes right through preparation. If you want to do something to your house, then the quality of the results will depend entirely on your due diligence on every detail. Let me be more specific. Start with an architect and you will instantly upgrade your end results from the beginning. An architect's expertise is invaluable in any home improvement project and too many times, people wing it without one and believe me, it shows. You can tell right away when you walk into a house that an armature was in charge at some point. An architect will protect you from some expensive and unsightly mistakes and give you ideas you never thought of that boost the enjoyment level of your home immensely as a result. Use their expertise. You will be glad you did.

Be prepared to do some serious amounts of shopping and decision making before you actually start the project. Once you settle on the design, make a list of items that you will need to purchase to complete the design. Create that spreadsheet for each room being worked on. Shop for the items you need, make your selections and record the costs of the items you picked out in the spreadsheet, before you even start. Remember that any items that are not picked out and priced will become "allowances" in the spreadsheet. They will be represented by a guesstimate of the cost of that line item if there is not a final selection made and could end up being unpleasant surprises. This gives you a very artificial total cost. If you have not finalized your selections for your plumbing fixtures, tile and cabinets, but still want to get started, you will be stunned unnecessarily. First, you will be stunned to identify the real cost of the items vs. the allowance figure you plugged into your spreadsheet prior to your final selection and second, you may be stunned to find out how long the item will take to be delivered once you order it.

Think ahead. Anticipate these potentially disruptive issues and solve them by selecting what you want BEFORE the work starts. I know you're busy, but if you want to renovate your house, you can't just wing it and hope for the best, get started and catch up as you get into it. I always marvel when I see people who are so eager to get things done to their house, but so detached from helping the progress because they just don't *feel like* looking at (for example) countertop slabs today to make a decision, they would much rather play tennis and sit by the pool... You shake your head, but there is nothing you can do about it if the homeowner is not in the mood to get things done. The bottom line: Be in the mood to get things done, until they're in fact, done. Then go play tennis...

You have to stay committed to the project until its conclusion if you want to finish in a reasonable time frame. You have to be prepared to make decisions, make selections, not hold anyone up and just keep going. When something changes because you asked for it in a contract, you need to sign off on it promptly when the revised contract "change order" is presented to you and keep track of those change orders in a folder.

On the subject of safety, keep your small children off an active jobsite. That is the only way to prevent injuries with 100% success. Any time you bring really young kids to a jobsite, there are enormous risks to them and to the workers. Just innocently catching their little foot on the wrong power cord or air hose could cause a carpenter to cut something or nail gun something he didn't intend to--including his hand. You certainly don't want your child injuring themselves either. If you are on the jobsite, you will be engrossed in the activity and not engrossed in your child's whereabouts. This is a bad idea for everyone involved. Keep them safe, keep them off the jobsite.

Be realistic about your budget in the first place. Discuss your goals with some qualified people like a good local General Contractor (whom you have properly vetted) and bounce your goals and your budget off him. Ask local building inspectors and local architects. Ask your friends and neighbors what their renovation work cost if they are comfortable sharing that information. The ballpark idea of cost is what you need, not down to the penny, mind you. That way, you can determine if you want to actually pay for and begin work on a design. Then, you can bid it out, which is the only precise way to calculate costs down to the penny. If you want a WOW kitchen, but only have $3,000 to spend, you either have to start saving more money or learn how to build great cabinets yourself...so you have to start out with a realistic idea of your budget to begin with.

Move out of your house if you are having extensive work done to your house. It is too much stress on your family and you, if you don't. If your utilities will be temporarily disconnected, if your furnace and air conditioning will be off for a while, if your house will be open to the elements except for some temporary plywood here and there, if there will be extensive drywall work sanded down or hardwood flooring sanded down, you don't want to be there. Move out, don't subject yourself or your family to that. Find a cheap rental somewhere close and live comfortably and let the work get accomplished. It is a colossal mistake to try to "save money" and have your belongings and clothing covered in drywall dust each day. It gets everywhere. Anyone who tells you they will simply "put some plastic up" to prevent it is just pulling your chain because so many people think that's a real solution. If you have a furnace, it will circulate the dust everywhere. If the workers have to go in and out of the plastic covered area, they will track dust and stir up dust in the process. Plastic makes people "feel" better, but doesn't actually do much to effectively trap dust.

Speaking of furnaces, it's important to keep your furnace filter changed 1-2x per month during any construction. Drywall and demolition dust can clog your furnace blower, so you have to protect it. It's best to just not run it at all during the heavy sanding and demolition stages. Therefore, it's always best to rent a place for a couple months during some projects. It's an expense, but you can find people with empty houses for sale which are empty because they moved away. They are more than happy to have some rental income each month for however many months you need to stay, provided the house does not sell. Take advantage of this reality all around you right now. Many of my clients have and it will be much easier on you too if you do!

Visit the jobsite and look around each day. You need to watch the progress each day an set a tone that you will be there each day, no matter what. If you are not visible, things can slide into mediocrity pretty fast, so be there each day observing, checking quality and discussing the details of the job as they unfold with the subcontractors and anticipating the next stage of the project and what they might need next to keep going. You are the problem solver, the facilitator, the communication hub for lots of people who need to cooperate together to complete the work. There is no substitute for being there, besides being there! You'll see. Thinking like a General Contractor means being on the jobsite every day, no matter what.

Be on the jobsite *especially* when items are being delivered. Check for damage the moment they lift it off the truck and be ready to send it right back if there is an issue. Or, snap a digital picture and email it so the company can send out the appropriate person to repair it.

Keep a shop vac handy and some micro fiber rags too. Especially as you near the final tasks of a job. There will always be some last minute messes to clean up and you can ruin some finishes with a dirty, wet work boot that smudges a tile or some sawdust that does not get cleaned up promptly and gets ground into the tile or hardwood floor. After a long hard journey, don't let something get damaged near the finish line! Watch for messes to clean up immediately when you are near completion.

As is the case with most things in life, a little common sense goes a long way, so use common sense in every matter that concerns your jobsite. The more you interact with all of the people that we suggested, the more you will learn. Be respectful and appreciative of their time and you will, in return, receive an overwhelming amount of helpful, free advice. You will also be in an even better position to take on the next challenge you face on the road to improving your house.

I hope these concepts helped you in some small way to take charge of your own project and to start achieving your home improvement goals with a more knowledgeable and practical approach. I sincerely wish you the very best of luck as you work toward your dreams for your house. Remember, *you* are the difference in making any project run more smoothly and more successfully. Here's to success-!

Acknowledgements

Who inspires me? It would be a shorter list to say who doesn't inspire me. That being said, this is for my late Dad, who built a business by himself which lasted 40 years until he sold it, by years of working brutally hard and maintaining a nonnegotiable integrity. His favorite witticism, "Always tell the truth. That way, you'll never have to struggle to remember what you said." His wife, Peg Dillon, was as much a mother to me as my late mother Therese and I will never forget her taking the time to personally visiting my jobsites...well into her eighties. She continues to inspire me in more ways than I can express. To Lori Anderson, who is, without a doubt, the most lovely and wonderful woman on earth in every way and proves it each day to us all. To my brother Bob, a brilliant engineer responsible for amazingly complex construction projects, but who's always interested in mine. To Hymen Childs, my friend and a legend among broadcasters, who charted his own course all the way to the top and remains there today, but as a real gentleman, always uncomfortable talking about his accomplishments. To all of the clients who trusted me when I said I would take care of them and took my word for it. I can't place a value high enough on the honor of your trust in me. To my brother Jack, who always helps me remember how many great things are right in front of me as he often marvels about the simple things that he really appreciates. His glass is always half full and he makes me realize mine is too. To my friend, Tim O'Brien, who is always the smartest guy in the room, but especially when it's just Tim and me in the room, but he never lets anyone know it. In addition to his sincere fascination with people, he also happens to be one of the most respected investigative reporters, most brilliant editors, most entertaining authors, and one of the most sincerely humble guys that I know. His daily adventures always pale mine, but he is always more interested in mine. His brother Michael O'Brien has helped me in more ways than I can count and they each have the same gleam in their eye as their father, the late Arthur O'Brien, an old friend and neighbor of my Dad's. Both men, may they rest in peace, inspired me with their World War II combat bravery, each returning home to build their own businesses, starting with nothing but their own determination while raising large families and quietly radiating their signature, old school humility...the kind of rare humility that only people who have achieved something genuinely great by their own refusal to give up, seem to all radiate. That's who inspires me...

Made in the USA
Columbia, SC
19 October 2018